PATRICK'S CORNER

May the Roads rise up to meet you;
May the Wind be always at your back;
The Sun shine warm upon your face;
The Rains fall soft upon your fields;
And,
Until we meet again,
May God hold you in the
Hollow of His Hand.

An Irish blessing

"May you be in Heaven a half an hour
before the divvil knows you're dead!"

An Irish blessing

PATRICK'S CORNER

Seán Patrick

PELICAN PUBLISHING COMPANY
Gretna 1992

To Kathleen: My heart and my love. For your understanding and your courage. For your own dedication and for being you. What better gift could a father have?

To Shawn Cunningham: My dear godson. May you stumble onto God's path and may it lead you to glory. So much like your godfather . . . even if your family didn't spell your name right!

To Pat: Especially for you . . . an Irishman's delight!

Library of Congress Cataloging-in-Publication Data

Patrick, Seán.
    Patrick's corner / by Seán Patrick.
      p. cm.
    ISBN 0-88289-878-7
    1. Irish Americans—Great Lakes Region—Biography. 2.
Catholics—Great Lakes Region—Biography. 3. Patrick,
Seán. 4. Patrick family. 5. Great Lakes Region—
Biography. I. Title.
F358.2.I6P38   1992
977'.0049162022—dc20
[B]   91-33634
                                                 CIP

Manufactured in the United States of America

Published by Pelican Publishing Company, Inc.
1101 Monroe Street, Gretna, Louisiana 70053

Contents

Preface

WHAT FOLLOWS IS THE STORY of the Patrick family. They are not unique for their space in the chronology of time, although it may seem odd to those of this generation to find a family this large who got along on so little.

Nor are they unique for their closeness, their interdependence, or their open affection, one for the other.

The Patricks, left by God as a family with one parent—a matriarch, at that—shortly after the birth of the youngest child, existed in material poverty. They inhabited, for many years, a small, two-bedroom apartment in the tenement district of a major northeastern city on the shores of one of the Great Lakes. Their neighborhood, like most neighborhoods of such cities, was identified by nationalities. Old World tradition abounded but Americanization occurred in spite of that.

Their story is told through the voice of Seán, the "gosoon" (Gaelic for baby or little child) of the family. It was Seán who had the privilege of benefitting from the wealth of his five older brothers. It wasn't material wealth, but a wealth of wisdom and caring which was passed unconditionally by Tommy, Billy, David, Kevin, and Danny to the youngest of the family.

The compressed neighborhood of Seán's childhood has given way, through the miracle of modern transportation and technology, to the expanded world of the shopping mall, the computer, and the television set. Seán's world was bounded by the distance one could comfortably travel on foot or on the city streetcar. Seán's experience of people was limited to the Hughes, the Weinsteins, the Spitzers, the Orlandos, and the others who served the community in their family groceries, bakeries, and meat markets.

And Seán's pride was born from the Patricks, who with their gifts nourished his soul as well as his body:

11

From Tommy . . . strength and dependability;
From Billy . . . flexibility and integrity;
From David . . . a love of learning and compassion;
From Kevin . . . a sense of humor and a ready smile;
From Danny . . . love.
. . . and from Mama . . . uncompromised dignity.

To all of the above:

From Seán-o . . . gratitude.

Shoeshine

ALL OF US WORKED ALMOST as soon as we were able. The positions we held were not exactly what one would consider real jobs by today's standards. But, for us, it was work and we did it with a vengeance.

I was born shortly after the Great Depression, the youngest of six boys. Daddy died soon after my birth and our mother was left with the unenviable task of trying to provide for us. In those days, the value of a woman's work was not fairly reflected in the pay envelope. She did "day work" and was able to pay the rent for the small apartment we lived in, huddled together in collective patience, two boys to a bed, three beds to the room barely large enough to accommodate one.

As each of us reached our two-digit birthdays, we became Associate Breadwinners. We had to if we wanted a little money to jingle in our pocket or to spend at the neighborhood movie theater on Saturday.

Local newspaper routes were generally conceded to be the sole property of the Patrick boys. We also held the monopoly on the sought-after position of clean-up boy at the local live poultry store on the corner of our street. That was a thirty-five cents per hour job! These jobs passed from Patrick to Patrick as age moved my brothers on to greater and more lucrative pastures.

Danny, the brother just senior to me, had the attractive job of "hawking" the evening newspaper on the busiest corner in town. This was a crosstown bus and streetcar exchange and, in the days before everyone had at least one car on the road and another in the garage, streetcars and busses were the major forms of transportation for the working public.

Every weekday, at precisely 5 P.M., Danny would position himself midway between the streetcar island and the bus shelter. He would stand there in glory with a paper raised high over his head and a bundle of papers under his left

13

arm. His voice was penetratingly Irish as he hawked the headlines. The pile of papers at his feet quickly dwindled and the bulge of nickels in his pocket swelled his short pants to bursting as men and women alike attacked him to get their daily ration of world and city affairs.

I had to work my way up to that exalted position. Danny would hold that until Kevin moved to the poultry store, vacating his home delivery route.

When I reached my tenth birthday, it was time for me to become the Patrick of the Shoeshine Stand.

The shoeshine stand was the least desirable of our family businesses for a number of reasons. First, it was uncomfortable. The shine boy knelt on the concrete sidewalk as the customer, leaning against Chris's Barber Shop wall, placed one foot after the other on the shine box footpad.

Secondly, the business was seasonal. Our harsh northern winters closed the stand from November until April. Rainy weather also precluded our business until the skies had cleared and the puddles had disappeared from the streets.

Lastly, the shine boy didn't make a lot of money. Three or four shines a day were about the best I could realize at the bus stop. Of course, the thirty or forty cents was almost pure profit. Ten cents a shine was the going rate and we had to remain competitive. The Skullys tried a fifteen-cent shine on their corner and almost went out of business. It's a cut-throat world!

My ten-cent shine soon matched the legends established by my predecessors: Tommy, Billy, David, Kevin, and Danny. I had my "regulars"—gentlemen who would stop a couple of times a week to get their brogans shined up. Fridays were busy, too.

Mr. Munstein was something else. He was my most regular customer. Day after day, week after week, Mr. Munstein would plant his foot on my stand at precisely five-thirty. He got off the Number 28 bus and came directly to Patrick territory. First, he would buy his paper from Danny and then move to my station. If a customer was being shined, he would wait patiently until I had finished, reading the front page of his newspaper carefully.

When it was his turn, Mr. Munstein would advance slowly, look at the toes of both shoes, and invariably exclaim that the city dirt was going to drive him to the poorhouse if he wanted neat shoes.

I took special pains with Mr. Munstein's worn shoes. I buffed them to a lustre with a real badger brush and then, using my best shine rag, I would "crack shine" them to a near mirror finish, popping my shine rag like an artist.

When I had finished, Mr. Munstein would step back and carefully look over the job. First the right shoe, then the left. I agonized during these moments.

Finally, he would reach in his pocket and draw out a thin Liberty dime and hand it to me ceremoniously.

"Always do your very best work," he would say, "because it will show your character."

He would then fold the paper under his arm and walk down the avenue towards his home.

In the winter months, Mr. Munstein did the unthinkable. He would appear at our apartment every evening and ask if it would be too much trouble to have a shoeshine. Mama would call me and I would take Mr. Munstein to the kitchen and shine his shoes. He always refused the cup of coffee Mama offered him, although on one very cold evening he did have a cup of hot chocolate with me at our kitchen table.

Early in my second year as shine boy, Mr. Munstein stopped coming. I looked for him to exit the Number 28 but to no avail. Finally, after a week or so of bus watching, I got up the courage to ask Don, the driver of Number 28.

"He died, Seán," Don said, "in his sleep."

Don told me that Mr. Munstein had lived with his sister on Forest Street.

"No pain . . . just slipped away. . . ."

My mood was somber when I told Mama and my brothers about my best customer.

"You know, Seán," Mama said, "his supply of dimes wasn't as big as you boys think. Mr. Munstein was very poor. His business failed during the Depression. He lost everything and lived with his sister so that he wouldn't have to go on welfare. He watched everything he spent and always said that he would never make a bad investment. He must have thought that you boys were a good 'investment' to make. He was a real friend to you all."

I thought about that later that night. Danny was sleeping soundly, making those soft whistling noises we kidded him about. I snuggled up next to my brother for the warmth of a human touch and thought about Mr. Munstein . . . and his dimes for the shoeshine, and his daily nickel for a paper from Danny.

I thought about my "friend" and was sorry I had never called him that. But he probably wouldn't have expected me to.

I hoped that I wouldn't wake Danny as my young body shook from my sobs as I wept for my loss.

The Garden

WHEN MAMA WAS UPSET, she prayed. When she was happy, she prayed. Whenever or whatever the occasion, Mama would pray. I am sure that heaven must have some sort of record of fervent prayers, a book or some scroll on which the serious prayers of good people are marked down. I'm sure, too, that Mama must hold some sort of special mention in that book or scroll because of her non-stop practice of praying over everything and anything.

She even prayed for a bird once. I remember that very clearly. The bird had flown in through our apartment window on a warm day and was valiantly trying to find its source of exit without causing too much commotion in the Patrick household.

For the non-Irish among us I must here make perfectly clear that a bird in the house (unless caged and fed regularly—a pet) is not a welcome occurrence. The superstitious Irish believe that it is a portent of death and that someone will die soon—someone near and dear, no less.

Well, Kevin chased the bird all around the apartment with the broom, trying to guide it to the open window. Instead, it found the closed one and smashed into it with, we thought, the force of a Grumman Avenger dive-bombing a foreign vessel during the recent unpleasantness called Midway.

The poor thing hit the window and dropped like a weight onto the linoleum floor, where it lay almost completely still. Its wing twitched and Kevin immediately picked it up and cradled it in his cupped hands.

"Cor! Mama, I think the poor bugger's about got it all over now!"

Kevin really was tender-hearted, in spite of his prior efforts to mimic an ax murderer with the broom moments before.

Mama, who had been crossing herself non-stop since the

17

chase began, immediately began a rapid-fire petition in Gaelic for the bird. This was followed by a series of Gaelic mutterings which I am certain were for the person, or persons, who would follow this bearer of death to Eternity. She stood in the doorway of the kitchen with her hands clasping her rosary beads, tears for the bird and for our pending misfortune in her Irish eyes.

I don't know why Mama carried her rosary beads everywhere she went because I rarely remember her saying the Rosary except in church. In the sacred edifice the beads would swiftly pass through her fingers and her silent lips would flutter with the praise of the Mother of God even during Monsignor Hanratty's sermons.

Anyway, she always carried her rosary beads in her apron pocket and would fish them out on any occasion which demanded prayer, even if the prayer had nothing to do with the Rosary.

Habit, I imagine. Or a sort of physical reminder that she was doing something sacred.

"Her" prayer, the one I remember most, was specific and was in Gaelic.

> *"Dia cuir anns dom na cinnteach ris fuloing ni mi chan urrainn ceist na morachd ris ceist ni mi is urrain agus na eolach ris fios na difrioce!"*

The throaty Gaelic would roll from her lips with a unique cadence which made even the guttural sounds seem musical. It was her "all occasion" petition to God.

In later years I would learn that the prayer was not hers. It had been around for a long time and was known as "The Serenity Prayer." I myself would use it frequently in connection with a lifestyle I would adopt. I still use it several times each day . . . more on some days than on others, but still every day. It means:

> *"God, grant me the Serenity to accept the things I cannot change;*
> *The Courage to change the things I can; and*
> *The Wisdom to know the difference."*

"Seán-o! Keep quiet for a minute! Mama's in her garden!" was a phrase which was often directed to this youngest son by one of his five older brothers. It meant that my usual rantings or boisterous invectives were disturbing Mama's prayers for some happening, happy or sad, which had found its way into the Patrick apartment.

Mama's "garden" was in her mind. I had the temerity to ask her about it one time. Her explanation not only made sense, it has given me a direction which no texts or teachers have been able to match.

"Me garden is all in here," she said, tapping her breast to indicate her heart. "I go there in me prayers to Almighty God or to His saints in Heaven. 'Tis a beautiful garden, indeed. So orderly and sweet smellin'. The rows are green and the potato leaves are at the rustlin' stage. The long pathways are bordered with the wild shamrocks which none dare pull for fear of offendin' the Wee People. The shamrock flowers are so white and Saint Patrick himself is there. . . ."

Mama had been raised in the country. She told us of the meager diet consisting largely of potatoes and occasional mutton from a family sheep. She mentioned the freshness of the vegetables from their family garden and told of how, after working the day in the coaleries, her father and brothers would spend the twilight hours tending the small patch which provided such bounty for the O'Hickey table.

"In my mind's eye and in the seat of me heart I return to that garden when I pray," she went on, "because there's a peace and a lovin' that these walls don't give . . . even though we have our own peace and lovin' within them."

Mama was called "Kate" by everyone else who knew her. Her physical stature was small, barely five feet tall and always at just about 100 pounds. Her hair was raven black and when the grey arrived it belonged there. Tommy, Billy, Kevin, Danny, and I all inherited the black hair. David, who took after the daddy I never knew, was the "redhead" of the family. But David was truly "Mama's boy" if we said that we had one among us.

Mama's translation (for our benefit) of the "Serenity Prayer" was a bit different from the one I would later learn. The meaning was the same, though.

"It means this," she once told us. "God, put into me the Certainty to suffer a thing I cannot change; the Sense of Greatness to change the things I can; and the Knowledge of the Heart to know the difference!"

I don't know how she moved with "Certainty" to face the unknown when Daddy was killed in an accident in the railroad yards where he labored to provide for us. I'm sure there must have been many moments of sincere trepidation as she envisioned raising six boys, ages one through six, by herself in a time of economic chaos in her adopted land. The discouragement must have been frequent, especially at first when none of us was able to assist except in childish ways. Yet, in all of my years with Mama, I never sensed hesitation.

"The Sense of Greatness." What a unique and beautiful way to tell of the courage of this woman who "changed the things" that she could by washing other people's clothes and ironing them to razor creases on the ever-standing ironing board of my childhood. It also speaks of the "courage" of accepting and receiving from others such kindnesses as the occasional chicken from the live-poulterers at the corner of our street, given in love to "save it from going to waste, Mrs. Patrick. Killed one too many today and the weekend ice won't keep it."

"I thank you, Mr. Blum. It's sure a treat for me boys to have a chicken now and again. God bless you, Mr. Blum."

Oh, Mama ate the chicken, too. A wing.

"That's all the carin' for chicken I have. You boys best eat it before Mr. Blum thinks we don't appreciate it!"

Later, when we could watch out for each other and she could leave the apartment, Mama would clean other people's houses and then return to our small apartment to pick up after six active and generally thoughtless boys whom she lived for.

"Knowledge of the Heart" was something Mama had. I suppose she made mistakes in judgment and lost her "cool"

20

on occasion. I'm sure of it, in fact. I just don't remember those times.

What I remember is her standing by the kitchen stove with her chipped mug of tea in her left hand and her right hand in her apron pocket . . . fingering her ever-present rosary beads.

Mama didn't need words to pray with. She used them, of course, but she really didn't need them. Like Theresa of Avila she was content to worship God with a scrub brush or an electric iron. She worshipped God with a quick kiss on the forehead of one or all of her sons. She worshipped God by stepping forth in her "Sense of Greatness" that she was doing what must be done; in her "Certainty" that some things must simply be borne; and in her "Knowledge of the Heart" that her choice—coupled with the faith that an all-loving God watched over her and her brood—would be the right one for the moment in time she was living in.

Many mornings Mama walked to St. Columbkille Church with Danny and I for the 5:45 A.M. Mass. Danny and I went because we were on the servers' list for that week at that unholy hour; Mama, because she needed those early morning moments in her "garden," undisturbed by the rest of the tenement world around us.

There, like the potatoes abounding and rustling in the soft and damp breeze of Ireland . . . with the velvety delicacy of the triune leaves of the wild shamrock caressing the borders of her paths . . . Mama could stand before the Throne and approach it with familiarity to draw the strength for another day of doing her, and His, work.

Many, many years later Danny would send me a parchment, on which had been penned by a professional—and very expensive—calligrapher, Mama's prayer in Gaelic. He knew how much it had come to mean to me and how I used it daily.

"Dan-o?" I poked my brother under the blanket which we shared.

"What, Seán-o?"

"Know where I was today?"

21

"I know where ye were. In school, just like me. Then we were at Patrick's Corner. I sold the news and you shined three pairs of shoes . . ."

"No, Dan-o! Where I was by meself!"

Kevin chimed in from his and David's bed.

"Tell us, Seán-o. The suspense is killin' me an I've an exam in the school tomorrow!"

"I was in Mama's garden today!"

Silence.

"Seán-o?" It was David's voice this time. David, the intellectual, the introvert, the gentle Patrick. . . .

"What, David?"

"I'm glad you found Mama's garden. I go there often meself."

Mutterings of agreement from the rest. I know we were all quietly lying on our backs with open eyes, staring at the dark ceiling of our common bedroom.

"I liked it there, David . . ."

Danny put his arm around my shoulder and kissed my cheek.

"Mama made the garden for all of us, baby brother," he said to me.

"Do you think we'll ever see each other there, David?" I asked in my twelve-year-old curiosity and simplicity.

"When it's time, Seán-o. When it's time."

I still go to Mama's garden. Regularly.

I haven't seen Tommy, or Billy, or David, or Kevin, or even Danny there, yet.

But I feel them there. And I feel Mama there, gone these long years to the garden to stay.

Someday I'll be there among the green with the Irish mist dampening my hair and I'll look around and see Tommy advising someone how to do something a better way. Billy will be there and he'll be talking shop with Kevin—both professional firemen. David will be tending the plants, carefully avoiding treading the shamrocks along the paths. Danny? He'll be holding my hand so that my clumsy feet don't step where they shouldn't. But I won't resent it. He's held my hand for more years than he'll ever know.

We'll all look up and see Mama . . . Kate.

She'll be fingering her rosary beads and will be happy because her garden will be forever and the seeds she planted will be strong and true.

"Dia cuir anns dom na cinnteach ris fuloing ni mi chan . . ."

The Gipper

LIKE EVERYTHING ELSE in our family of six boys who were very close in age, sports and activities followed a set progression. Tommy would start a thing, Billy would be the next to do it, David would succeed Billy, and so on, down the line. It was an unspoken maxim that what one Patrick started, the rest would follow . . . and succeed in.

Sports were certainly no exception. Tommy was a natural athlete, tall and well proportioned. He had the quick mind of a strategist and the swift movements of a well coordinated artist. He was, as I have already said, "a natural."

We all attended the same elementary school. Saint Columbkille had eight grades and, usually, most of them had a Patrick in them until we began graduating and moving on to the Holy Redeemer High School (Holy Moley, we used to call that place, irreverently).

As we reached the sixth grade, it was expected that we would try out for, and make, the school football team. Our town had a very large contingent of parochial schools and the CYO (Catholic Youth Organization) league was truly a thing which, we felt, would rival the present NFL in prestige and power.

Unfortunately, unlike Tommy or Billy—or David, or Kevin or Danny—this Patrick was not a natural athlete. I played, of course, with the family in our "touch" football games in Daily's Field. That was fun. But the CYO league was sheer cutthroat mayhem. Still, it was my duty as a Patrick—so I was brutally informed by the above-named five—to try out for . . . and make . . . the team.

This I did. I did both, that is. I survived the rigorous planned torture of the three days of tryouts with a little dignity and was finally allocated a spot on the team. Coach Farrell didn't give me the accolades given to some of the Manning boys, who were all super jocks, but he did say that I would be "something" on the team.

I felt an awkward pride standing in my hand-me-down underpants to be fitted for the green and gold of Saint Columbkille's Mighty Lions.

My sixth-grade and seventh-grade years were not spectacular. In fact, the team would have played well without me. I was allowed to play when we were several touchdowns ahead and the morale of the opposition was at its lowest ebb. But I did play.

Coach Farrell thought that I would be a good offensive end. Offense, because I was too small to take the battering the defensive line had to endure; end, because I had no—zero—backfield finesse or skills at all. This was acceptable because Kevin was one of the most remembered ends in the hallowed history of Saint Columbkille. He once caught four touchdown passes in a CYO championship game, setting records that Knute Rockne would have been envious of.

When I was thirteen, and in the eighth grade, the action picked up a little. Sheer exposure to the game as coached by Francis X. Farrell gave me some confidence and a smattering of ability. True, I wasn't always the starting offensive end, but I usually played a good piece of every game.

Saint Columbkille, as usual, turned out a formidable gridiron crew in my eighth-grade year. We rolled over the less fortunate opponents with an ease which we took for granted. We were, as we liked to tell ourselves and as our parents boasted in the pubs, a "cinch" for the league championship, an honor which had eluded us for the last two years in the last games of the season.

On the Sunday which counted—Championship Day—we arrived early at the St. Vitus High School field and suited up for the big game. Coach Farrell was at his Rocknean finest. We had the "Get one for the Gipper" speech at least twice before we made our debut on the field.

Halfway through the first quarter, Seamus O'Donnell twisted his ankle and was helped off the field. Seamus was the starting right end. His ankle swelled rapidly in spite of the ice Coach Farrell packed on it. Seamus had bought the long, slow walk to the showers. This meant only one thing for the Patrick boys who sat in a long, grim line in the bleachers. Seán-o would see some real action for at least one time in his career as a Saint Columbkille Lion.

I held my own for the greater part of the game. Coach Farrell wisely refrained from telling the quarterback to "let the RE take it over the chalkline," as he was wont to say. I did my job blocking and, since I had developed somewhat as puberty approached, was able to fend off the defensive linemen the Saint Vitus team threw at me.

Saint Vitus was a tough team, no doubt about it. They held us scoreless for the first half and we reciprocated in kind. In the third quarter, they scored on a piddling little pass over on the left sideline. This fired up the Lions and "Irish" Kennedy literally ran through the entire Saint Vitus line to score a few plays later.

As many championships go, the game became a real cliff-hanger. The rest of the third quarter was pure bloody battle. The fourth quarter was sheer desperation, each team vying valiantly but not really gaining any advantage over the other. The minutes ticked by relentlessly, and this was in the day before "sudden death" overtimes. You won, you lost, or you tied. Losing was not in the Lions' vocabulary . . . or so Francis X. Farrell told us.

Saint Vitus had the ball and our offensive team squatted on the bench waiting for our chance to get the ball back and do something with it. I concentrated hard, muttering Hail Marys one after the other in an endless string of petitions. Suddenly, I realized that I was not alone on my end of the bench.

The sachet smell was unmistakable. I didn't even have to turn my head to know that one of God's More Sacred Creatures was seated on the bench next to this hapless right end. A nun!

I turned my head ever so slightly and caught sight of the florid and furrow-browed face of Sister Saint Patrick, or Pat the Hatchet, as we referred to our eighth-grade teacher. It was rumored that she had trained to be the first woman prizefighter in Ireland but that she had killed an opponent in the ring and had joined the convent in reparation for this horrible offense against the laws of God and man.

With quiet dignity and the stride of a railroader, she rose from the bench and walked directly to Francis X. Farrell, who was agonizing from the sidelines. She spoke a few words to him and, before he could say anything back, turned and marched back to take her seat next to the last Patrick the Lions would ever see.

She sat down and I automatically attempted to provide a comfortable space between this nun and myself. Before I could shift my small backside, she reached out and put her arm around my shoulders and pulled me close to her starched coif.

"Seán," she said quietly, "when the offense goes back in, the quarterback is going to lob a short pass to you. You'll have to get around their lineman and turn quickly to see it coming. When you get it . . ."

"But, S'ter!" I began to protest.

"When you get it," she continued as if my voice had been nothing more than a bothersome insect during her prayer time, "when you get it, turn and run like hell!"

With that said, she released my shoulder and sat back. I could see her hand, almost buried in the volume of cloth which made up her skirt, expertly fingering her rosary beads.

The Saint Vitus eleven made no progress and had to punt. We got the ball on our own forty-yard line and the offense went spiritedly back to the field.

We huddled. Frankie Manning, our quarterback, called the play I had been dreading. My mind conjured up images of Coach Farrell damning the day he agreed to coach for the school Sister Saint Patrick taught in. Frankie clapped his hands and we lined up for the snap.

The ball snapped back and we charged forward. Fortunately, the defensive player assigned to "take me out" had gotten to the point where he didn't consider me a serious threat. I sidestepped him and trotted in back of him, keeping a few feet inside the sideline. I turned and saw the ball coming directly at me.

Frankie was a good quarterback and he hit me "right on the numbers." Sister Saint Patrick's prayers must have shaken up some of the saints in Heaven because the ball actually stayed in my hands. For an instant I was overjoyed to realize that I hadn't dropped the ball. Then harsh reality closed in. I remembered her instructions and turned on my toes to "run like hell!"

I really think that the Saint Vitus defense was too shocked to believe that the "Patrick kid" had the ball. There was no instant pursuit and I reached the goal line seconds ahead of my nearest pursuer. The stands—our stands—went wild. I could hear my brothers' voices above all the rest. "Shaaaaawwwwwwwnnnn!"

The rest of the game was fuzzy and somewhat uneventful. We had several minutes left to play and no one did anything to threaten the other. By the time the gun went off to end the game, my head was spinning and my shoulderpads and rear end had been slapped and patted by my fellow team members so much that I felt like a friendly punching bag. "Way to go, Seán-o!" was the phrase of the afternoon. The champions marched off to the showers amid parents and classmates clamoring to let the world know that Saint Columbkille School COULD NOT BE BEATEN!

As I trudged towards the locker room I saw the huge form of black and white parting the crowd, much the same as Moses must have parted the Red Sea. Students and parents alike faded before her as Sister Saint Patrick, looking for all the world like a Sequoia in a pine forest, commanded that the world make way for her.

She motioned for me to stop and I did. Pushing the last opposition out of her way, she took hold of my jersey and pulled me close to her again. She looked directly into my eyes and, for the first time—and the last time I can remember—I saw affection shining.

"Seán . . . you did it!" she said with pride.

Then, bending over until her face was almost touching mine, she whispered in my ear. Her rich Irish brogue was pure music to me, for I was the only one who heard what she said.

"You did it . . . Gipper!"

I stood for a second, mouth open, eyes wide, watching her "sail" off into the crowd. Then my face broke into a ridiculous grin so wide I expected my freckles to drop off.

She was right—but only halfway. *I* didn't do it. *We* did it!

The Courtship

NOTHING IS VERY "PERSONAL" when many related persons live together. When one considers the fact that (*a*) I had five older brothers, (*b*) we all shared the same bedroom, closet, and chest of drawers, and (*c*) that all were very prideful of the fact that they were "raising the baby of the family," privacy and a personal life were virtual unknowns.

Such was the case, of course, with all the Patrick boys. We were very close in age and, as a result, lived for a long, long period of time together. All but Tommy wore hand-me-downs and, sometimes, these items of apparel would traverse all six before being designated as "trash." Winter coats, for instance. The old once-plaid macintosh with the zippered hood went through all of us. The only real difference was that the plaid gradually disappeared and the coat was a dirty maroon by the time it got to me. But I wore it.

I really think that I joined the United States Navy in order to get my own first-hand underwear. At least three Patricks wore the white cotton briefs before they reached me. By the time I was allotted the skivvies, a safety pin came with them because the elastic had lost its stretch during Danny's tenure with them.

When we finally got a telephone, some time after the Second World War, no conversation was completely unheard. I remember hearing the lives of my older brothers changed by the curt dismissal of the current girlfriend. I knew where the dates were going to take place and what movie they were going to see. Life had no surprises for a Patrick.

Kevin was the smart one. I can recall his making a date with Megan O'Neill. "I'll be a little late . . . I'll meet you in the second-to-last row. . . ." Kev would say. He was smart indeed. My other brothers always paid for their girlfriends' seat. Kevin met his in the theater after they had already paid for their own. His only out-of-pocket expense was the box of popcorn he would share with Megan. And I think he ate most of that, too.

Kev did this for years. I thought Megan was pretty dumb until the day she married my brother. Now she's making up for all of the tickets she had to pay for herself. Life is fickle.

The Patrick boys had a certain protocol. One didn't just announce that he was "dating." Mama had certain rules, and these were followed by all regardless of station or desire.

For instance, at thirteen it was permissible to take a girl to a birthday party in someone's home . . . provided that the "someone" was known and approved of by Mama. At fourteen, movies and the soda bar in the corner drug store were acceptable. When one reached fifteen, most of the barriers fell and it was O.K. to visit the girl at her home or to bring her home to our apartment. The front porch was then to be deserted by the rest of the boys. During the winter months, the kitchen saw many pretty colleens sitting at our oilcloth-covered table, sipping chocolate from one of our chipped mugs.

Real "dating" usually started at sixteen or better.

I had gone through the birthday party stage at thirteen. I had exactly two "dates" during that year. They were disasters because I got sick at the first one and she got sick at the second. In fact, the girl I took out both times was a distant cousin named Alice Maureen who was already committed to a life in the convent by her pious mother. (She did enter the convent after high school and stayed for almost a month.)

I don't think that a cousin, no matter how distant, counts as a date. So, one might say that I didn't date at all when I was thirteen.

Fourteen was a different story. I was "ready to go" and fantasized for months about my future as a romantic Irishman. I watched my brothers carefully, trying to absorb the enviable ease with which they carried themselves. I listened, in the privacy of our six-boy bedroom, to their stories of their "conquests" which, I now believe, were much akin to my own fantasies. Still, it was exciting.

31

I had been fourteen for almost a month when I got the courage to ask Patty Lennon to accompany me to the local theater for a Saturday evening "on the town." I had saved some money from my job as paper boy and was prepared to blow it all on Patty. The only fly in the ointment was that, as usual, word got out.

"Seán-boy!" Billy said at breakfast on Thursday, "Kev tells me that you've asked a girl out this weekend!"

I wilted. At that moment, I memorized the details of every dimple on each Rice Krispie in my bowl.

"Ah! Baby brother's joinin' the ranks of the Patrick men!" Tommy said, smiling slyly with his head thrown back and his eyes penetrating my body like knitting needles.

"He's takin' her to the movies at the Pearl," loose-lipped Kevin said with a full mouth. He had to repeat it twice to be sure that everyone—Mama included—heard it clearly and accurately.

"What's this, Seán?" Mama said from her usual position, drinking her cup of tea at the stove. "I didn't know that you were datin' already."

"I'm fourteen," I muttered to my Rice Krispies.

"What did you say, Seán? I didn't hear that."

"I'm fourteen, Mama." I said. "I'm the right age now."

"Indeed you are," she said, "Indeed you are. I almost forgot that my baby was fourteen already."

I hated the word "baby," but had gotten used to it, so it didn't sting so badly anymore.

I took some more friendly banter and thought that I had passed the test pretty well. Nothing more was said after that breakfast and I thought that the boys had forgotten all about my date and had become engrossed in their own social lives.

Saturday afternoon was a busy time in our household. We had the luxury of one bathroom. Mama wisely disappeared into Mrs. O'Malley's apartment for the greater part of the late afternoon. She knew that havoc would reign until at least six P.M. and wanted only the peace and quiet of Mrs. O'Malley's childless flat.

32

Our hot water heater, an obscene-looking monster with exposed rivets and a side-arm gas burner, stood in a corner of the bathroom. This provided about forty gallons of relatively hot water which, if rationed carefully by each user, would last for about three showers and, if he were lucky, for Tommy to shave with.

All Patrick boys were required to take "navy" showers. This consisted of getting in the tub and into the small round tent formed by the canvas curtain. The water was turned on and one got as wet as possible in as short a time as feasible. He turned the water completely off and soaped furiously while his body was still dripping. He was then allowed to turn the water on to rinse the Sunlight Soap off and to get his hair wet. A good palmful of Halo Shampoo was then rubbed into the hair and quickly rinsed off. A final instant under the stream of water was cut short by the next naked Patrick ordering that the ring of canvas be vacated before all the hot was gone.

Shaving (for Tommy, and eventually Billy), showering, and toothbrushing all took place simultaneously. I'm sure some modern choreographer would have been inspired by the movements of the six Patricks balleting their way to cleanliness and gentility.

On "my" Saturday—the day of my first date—I was given all of the consideration of the occasion. I was showered first. Kevin rubbed the Halo into my hair with a steady chatter about "groomin' Don Juan" for his tryst with his lady love. Tommy offered me his razor which, wisely, I declined. Danny, the brother closest to me in age, polished my hand-me-down wingtips.

I dressed under the close scrutiny of all my brothers. After changing trousers twice and finally borrowing a pair of almost-too-big gaberdine pants from Danny, along with a freshly pressed white shirt which Mama had hidden in her closet, I was ready to go and had passed the approval of the clan.

Mama stepped out of Mrs. O'Malley's apartment when she heard us leaving to give me a quick kiss (which I attempted to sidestep), and to tell me to have a good time. Kevin and Danny were going to the bowling alley where Kevin worked and walked me partway to Patty's apartment. Tommy, Billy, and David were going on dates of their own and disappeared in various directions.

My evening with Patty was a great success. She was ready when I got to her apartment and neither of us had seen the picture at the Pearl. I paid for the tickets (the girl at the box office knew all of us and smiled knowingly when I bought them), and I got us each a box of popcorn at the stand inside the theater. We sat about midway down the aisle and exactly in the center of the row.

Sometime, after the first seven or eight hours of the picture, I got the courage to kind of put my hand on Patty's. She didn't move hers and that's the way we sat through the rest of the movie. I breathed easier and smiled. I was actually enjoying myself.

After the show, we stopped at the drug store and had Cokes. I walked Patty home and made it well before her ten o'clock curfew.

I'd like to say that I kissed her goodnight, but I'd be lying.

"Seán-o!" The voice awakened me and I sat up a little in bed. Tommy, Billy, David, and Kevin were standing over me with their elven Irish smiles.

"Seán-boy! How did it go, your date?"

"Did you kiss her, Seán-o?" That from David.

Danny came out of the bathroom and sat on our bed looking for all the world like he was my protector.

"Let him go, guys! The bugger's all tuckered in!"

"Well," said Kevin, "at least tell us if you had a good time."

"Yeah, I had a real good time!" I muttered, smiling at their collective concern.

Danny reached over and roughed my hair up. Tommy rubbed my bare shoulder and smiled at me. Kevin and David were hanging up their clothes, but kept throwing knowing smiles my way. Billy came over to my bed and hugged me.

"You're a real Patrick man now, boy-o," he said, "datin' and all."

"'Night, guys," I said and crawled back in. Danny climbed in after me and we pulled the sheet over us.

"'Night, Casanova!" someone chimed in. I didn't know who Casanova was, but I figured it was a compliment.

Danny ruffled my hair again and put his arm around my shoulders.

At that moment I really felt the closeness of my brothers and how much they loved me as they watched me grow into manhood.

Life was super, and I felt good about it. I rolled over and slept instantly and peacefully, content in the belief that I was finally growing up.

The Weakness

OF ALL MY RELATIVES, not counting my mother and my five brothers, my favorite was Uncle Seán. I was named after him. He was a railroader and looked the part—big, burly, and Irish through and through.

When Uncle Seán came by our apartment, it was an occasion of pure joy for me. I would stand at the corner of his chair at the kitchen table and listen to him tell the tales of disaster and doom he gathered from his job as a foreman on the New York Central wreck salvage crews. Whenever an NYC train derailed or wrecked, it was Uncle Seán's crew that went out with a triple engine pulling the massive wrecker cars and flats loaded with equipment that could toss around weight that would make King Kong cringe at the very thought of lifting it.

My uncle never stayed very long. He would have the cup of tea Mama offered him and tell us the tales we longed to hear. Then, looking at his bulky railroad watch, he'd rise to his giant height and say, "Well, boy-o, I think I hear the grindin' of the wheels. Better get on back to the barns before they leave without me. Those boys couldn't lift a caboose with a full crane if I wasn't there to tell 'em how to do it."

He'd put his striped railroad hat on his shock of reddish curls and stride to the door with me on one side and Mama on the other. The rest of the Patricks followed in his wake like dolphins.

"Kate, take care of me boys," he'd say. Then, invariably, he'd turn to me and put his calloused hands on my thin shoulders.

"Seán-boy, keep our name proud. I love you, boy-o!"

And he'd be gone.

This did not happen often. At least, not often enough for me. I loved the visits, no matter how infrequent or how short they were.

36

After he went, Mama would cross herself and sometimes wipe her eyes with her apron. She very seldom said anything for a few minutes and my brothers wisely left her alone. They seemed to know something I did not.

Uncle Seán's visits were always different from the visits of my other uncles. When Uncle Jerry, Uncle Mike, or Uncle Joe came by, Mama would be more animated and converse more with them. Of course, they paid a lot more attention to her than did Uncle Seán. At these times, Mama would reach under the kitchen sink where she kept the soap powder and lift out the bottle of Kennedy's Irish Whiskey to pour a good couple of fingers for the visiting uncle. For Uncle Seán, though, it was always the cup of tea.

Uncle Seán was Mama's youngest brother and the only one who had never married. I don't think he had a home of his own. He seemed to live at "the barns," as the roundhouse was called. Here he had his world—loud, steamy, hot, and dirty. His crew was his family and his engine was his mistress. And Uncle Seán seemed to love the life he had chosen.

Sometimes I would lie on the bed Danny and I shared, even though it wasn't bedtime, and dream dreams of Uncle Seán's world. I would picture a vast train, miles long, in a crumbled heap . . . usually partly in a stream, with people running around in confusion. Then the wrecker crew would arrive with Uncle Seán at the throttle of the blurting and thrusting engine. He would lean out the cab window and people would realize that help had finally arrived. Calm would set in as Uncle Seán and his crew piled out of the engine and two cabooses.

I pictured myself at Uncle Seán's side, blaring out orders to the crew and pointing to the injured and maimed, sweat on my forehead and dirt on my rough hands. Two Seáns saving the NYC for the hundredth time!

As I grew older, the different treatment of my favorite uncle became more apparent to me. When I asked my brother, Tommy, about this, he sidestepped my question with an abruptness that told me that all was not well.

"Don't mind things like that, Seán-o," Tommy said. "It's none of our concern."

It was my concern. Uncle Seán and I shared the same name and he was my favorite uncle. It was Uncle Seán who always grasped my shoulders and planted a rough kiss on my forehead before he left. It was Uncle Seán who always looked around the kitchen and, if I was not in sight, would shout in his piercing, train-whistle voice.

"Where's my buck-o? Seán-boy! Where ye hidin'? Come out and see your old uncle!"

It was Kevin who finally gave me part of the answer.

Kevin and I were always very close. Not as close as Danny, who was only a year older than I was, but close just the same. Kevin was fifteen when I was just turning thirteen and he was the one who let me tag along when he went to the bowling alley where he worked or to watch him play stickball on a neighboring street.

If I ever needed answers to personal questions or needed a sage to confide in, it was usually Kevin I turned to.

"Well, it's kind of like this, Seán-o," Kevin said. "Uncle Seán has a sort of problem. It's 'the Weakness,' and it makes Mama sad."

"What's 'the Weakness,' Kev? Is it like bein' sick?"

"Kind of. It means that Uncle Seán has a love for the liquor. He drinks too much and sometimes does some pretty crazy things."

"Is that why Mama only gives him tea when he comes?"

"I guess so. She's awful worried about Uncle Seán. He's her baby brother, you know."

Kev always tried to give me an answer I could understand. I didn't fully understand what he was talking about, but at least I had part of the picture.

It would be all too clear, all too soon.

I vividly remember the day it happened. It started out to be a very normal school day for the Patrick boys. I was in the eighth grade at Saint Columbkille School. The rest of my brothers were in high school, except for Tommy, who worked full time at the butcher shop a block from our apartment.

38

When I got home from school, earlier than my brothers who were at Holy Redeemer High School, I got a glass of water and went to the kitchen to work on my arithmetic before I had to leave for my shoeshine corner. The door was unlocked but Mama wasn't in the kitchen like she usually was. The ironing board wasn't standing in its usual place in the center of the large kitchen. More alarming, the pot full of potatoes was not sitting on the back burner waiting for a friendly fire to cook them to their starchy glory.

I knew that something was wrong but figured that I'd better get to my arithmetic before I made matters worse.

Halfway through my mixed fraction exercise I heard someone come in the front door. The voices were soft and unfamiliar. I turned my head slightly, trying not to appear to be a "nibby nose," as I was so often accused of being. Mrs. Gallagher and Mrs. O'Brien were standing in our doorway.

"Seán! I didn't hear you come up the stairs," Mrs. O'Brien said.

"Where's Mama?" I asked. There was absolute alarm in my quivering voice and Mrs. O'Brien came quickly to me and put her arm around my shoulders.

"Your Mama's fine, Seán. She had to go out for a while. There's been an accident and her brother's been hurt."

I was trembling now. I heard the downstairs door slam and could hear the loud voices and heavy tread of four of my brothers as the Holy Redeemer Patricks returned from their day at school.

They burst in the front door and stopped as a man, looking at Mrs. Gallagher and Mrs. O'Brien and at me.

Danny came directly to me, fear in his eyes.

"Seán! Are you O.K., baby brother?"

"Your Uncle Seán has had an accident," Mrs. O'Brien began.

"Uncle Seán!" I gasped.

"He's at the Saint Vincent," Mrs. O'Brien continued. The "Saint Vincent" was the name by which we knew the local hospital, a mile and a half from our home. "Your mother's there now with him. You boys are to put the potatoes on and

39

go about your business."

How could I even think of "going about my business" when my favorite uncle was injured?

"Was he hurt on the train?" I asked Mrs. O'Brien.

"No, Seán. Your Mama'll tell you all about it. God help him. You have your own work to do and it'll take your mind off of it."

Danny and I went to Patrick's Corner, where he hawked the news and I shined a few pairs of shoes. I don't think that I did a very good job because my mind pictured Uncle Seán lying under white sheets with a platoon of doctors standing over him and nurses mopping his brow.

When we got home Mama was there. We found her sitting at the kitchen table with a steaming mug of tea in front of her and Mrs. Gallagher and Mrs. O'Brien on either side. Mrs. Gallagher held Mama's free hand in her own and I could see that Mama had been crying.

Mama didn't cry like other people. She didn't shake or sob or make any noise at all. She simply sat and tears would roll down her cheeks. Occasionally, she'd wipe her eyes delicately with a white handkerchief, but she never seemed to have to blow her nose or anything. It was a very bothersome way to cry, I felt. I would have preferred the more conventional way. I could have dealt with that better.

"Mama . . ." Danny said.

Mama turned and saw the two of us standing like candles in the kitchen. She pulled her hand free of Mrs. Gallagher and turned on her chair with her arms spread wide. We both rushed into them. She held us so tightly that our faces touched and I felt I would smother against Mama's breast.

"He's gone, boys," Mama said with a soft, soft voice. "Your Uncle Seán has gone to his reward."

She relaxed her hold on us and looked directly into my dark eyes.

"Ah, Seán! How you'll miss him, boy-o!"

I was crying by this time. Not the soft tears like Mama's. These tears rose from my very soul and flooded out in a torrent of shaking sobs. Mama held me for a few minutes.

40

When she felt I was quieter, she released me. Danny took me by my arm and led me to the bedroom. I lay on the bed crying while Danny sat by me stroking my neck and just being there.

Uncle Seán was waked in our front room. Many people came, most of them railroaders. They stood around in small groups talking quietly and then would disappear into the kitchen to snack on some of the bounty the neighbors had provided and to sip on the whiskey punch that rested in a large soup pan on the kitchen sideboard. Their conversation was predictably the same.

"In his long, narrow box tonight. Auld Seán's got it all over now . . ."

"Restin' with the saints and in the hollow of His hand . . ."

And the paper cups were raised again and again.

It wasn't until after the funeral when we were all back at our apartment that I learned the details of Uncle Seán's "accident."

I had heard smatterings of conversations at Aunt Helen's, where the after-funeral meal was served, but these only piqued my curiosity. I was still afraid to ask anything.

In our apartment, Tommy, Billy, and David gathered in a small knot talking quietly. Finally, Tommy broke away and said something to Danny. Then, somberly, he and Danny came over to the "baby" and took me by the arm.

"C'mon in the bedroom, Seán-boy. We got somethin' to talk about."

I followed Tommy and Danny into the bedroom. The others, standing quietly in the living room, watched us go. Tommy shut the door.

"Sit on the bed, boy-o. . . ."

I sat. Danny sat next to me. Tommy stood over me like a protecting angel.

"Uncle Seán died from 'the Weakness,' Seán-o. He drank too much and it made him kind of crazy. Once he started he couldn't stop and he became someone you wouldn't like to know."

"I'd always like Uncle Seán!" I protested.

41

"Quiet, boy-o! Listen to me. I'm tellin' you this because you got to know and you have a right to know. When Uncle Seán drank he became a monster. He was nasty and ugly. He was a fighter."

"He was the best fighter in the world!" I shouted.

"Seán-boy, Uncle Seán got killed in a bar fight. He was crazy and tried to hurt another man very badly. The bar owner had to shoot him."

I gasped. No heroic death trying to save lives in battered and wrecked railroad cars lying half in a river!

"It was 'the Weakness' that killed him, Seán. He was a fine, fine man when he didn't drink. A fine, fine man!"

I jumped up and threw myself at Tommy, arms flailing the air and small fists bouncing off the broad chest of my oldest brother.

Danny grabbed me from behind and pinned my slender arms to my sides. I was screaming something at Tommy but neither he nor I could make out the words I was saying.

Instead of hitting me back, Tommy held my head in both his hands and kissed me on the forehead like Uncle Seán used to do.

"Oh, me poor, poor boy-o! Seán-boy, it'll be alright, baby brother. It'll be alright."

When I had calmed, Mama stood in the doorway and motioned Tommy and Danny to leave the room. She sat next to me on the bed and told me tales of Uncle Seán in Ireland. How he had mastered soccer when he was only a boy like me, and "hurling," too. How he had worked on their parents' farm and dug peat for the kitchen fire. How he had gone to the mainland and mined coal to earn passage for him and his sister—my mother—to come to America to join Jerry and Michael and Joe. . . .

"Most important, Seán, he loved you and you loved him. He never came by here drinkin' because it was something he never wanted you to see. You, boy-o. He never wanted you to see.

"You're to remember him as you saw him, Seán. He was . . . inside . . . just exactly what you saw."

"I loved him, Mama."

"What did he always tell you, Seán-boy?"

"Mama?"

"Keep our name proud!"

"I will, Mama . . ."

I was O.K. after that. We had a late supper and sat listening to Amos and Andy. I was allowed to stay up until the older boys were told that it was time for bed.

"Seán-o?" David called from the bed he and Kevin shared when the lights were out and the sheets pulled over us.

"What, David?"

"Did you say your prayers tonight, boy-o?"

"'Course I did, David!"

"Did you remember to pray for Uncle Seán?" he asked.

"Sure I did!"

"So did I, Seán-boy . . ."

"Me, too," said Tommy . . . and Billy . . . and Kevin.

"Me, too, brother," said Danny, as he nudged me under the sheet.

"Keep the name proud!" I heard one of my brothers say from across the room. I think it was Tommy.

"I will!"

The Felon

AS FAR AS ANY OF US were concerned, there were only two policemen who counted for anything. They were the only two we ever saw in our neighborhood and, like us, they were part of the scenery.

Patrick Shaugnessy and Tony Marchetti were partners. They worked out of the local station house, which was across the street from Kornblum's Meats, where Tommy worked after finishing high school and before he went into the navy.

As partners, they were always seen together. They rode in the same black and white, they investigated the same crimes, they bowled on the same alleys with their wives on Thursday nights. One never thought of Pat without thinking of Tony in the same brainwave.

My relationship with these two minions of the law was very casual and, of course, unofficial. I felt a certain importance waving to them as they drove slowly by, eyes scanning the streets, doorways, and alleys for signs of evildoing. On Thursday evenings, when Kevin would let me come to the bowling alley to watch him set pins, I always walked by the horseshoe-shaped bench where Pat, Tony, and their wives sat, usually on alley nine. I'd wave and say a soft "Hi, guys!" and always felt a bit of exaltation when these important and powerful men would lift their eyes for an instant and recognize me by calling me by name.

The Patrick family's experience with the law was limited to the single time we called the police station to report that Billy, then fourteen, had been robbed of his collection money on his paper route. Billy had recognized his assailants as the notorious Kelly brothers from another neighborhood.

Both Pat and Tony (we called Tony "Tony Macaroni") arrived in a few minutes, got the information they required, and reappeared an hour later with the Kellys in their squad

44

car and Billy's money in their hands. Their very presence in our small apartment made me feel very small, indeed. I stood silently, looking at the handle of the huge pistol on Pat's hip and wondering how it would feel to be dressed in the blue uniform and to have all of those mysterious things hanging on my own gunbelt.

When I was eleven, my best friend . . . apart from my brothers, especially Danny, was a boy named Dickey Halloran. Dickey and I were in the same class at Saint Columbkille and he lived in a duplex on our street. For a long time we were inseparable.

Dickey was an only child whose father worked on the railroad like most of the working men in our neighborhood. He was an engineer and commanded a certain respect from all because of that position. In fact, he was a PASSENGER train engineer, which was more important still.

I used to like to go to Dickey's house after school during the months when my shoeshine stand stood idle because of the weather. We would go to his room and he would find the most amazing games and toys I had ever seen. His closet was jammed with things that I would dream about at Christmastime but never really saw except in the Western Auto catalog, which arrived about Thanksgiving.

We would play with Dickey's bounty until it was time for me to go home for supper. I was, I believe, a little jealous of my best friend's possessions, but never let this stop me from playing with them.

Shopping centers were a thing in the distant future when I was a boy. People relied on public transportation for exit from their neighborhoods, and so most of life revolved around one's own area and was limited to the three- or four-block area which was home. We had the few stores locally with which we dealt: the butcher, the grocery and, glory of glories . . . the dime store!

Mason's was a genuine five- and ten-cent store. Many things cost just that and all of us used to love to go in there and roam up and down the aisles looking at the merchandise we dreamed of having. There was a light coating of sawdust on the wooden floors and the ladies who worked behind the various counters kept a vigilant eye to make sure that our hands were clean before we touched anything.

My favorite place in the store, naturally, was the toy counter. Anyone could look at shoes or jackets or school supplies, but toys—*that* was something else! It was like being in Santa's workshop just prior to Christmas Eve.

Here, on a two-sided counter with a walkway for the clerk in between, lay treasures beyond imagining. I especially remember a shiny tin bulldozer with a real clock-spring motor. I pictured building great highways in the dust of our barren backyard, the roaring "Cat," with its genuine rubber treads, moving tons and tons of soft earth to make way for the procession of toy cars which would soon travel great distances at high speeds between our apartment yard and the Reillys' fence.

Like most parochial schools, Saint Columbkille observed a steady wealth of Catholic "feast" days and we got a day off of school. The "Publics," who were a great minority in our Irish neighborhood, suffered the ignominy of trudging to Lawn Elementary on those days while all we were required to do was to attend the Children's Mass in the parish church before going back home to luxuriate in the freedom only a Catholic kid can imagine, observing the feast of Saint Someone or Other while the Publics sweated over their fractions and decimals.

On one such feast day . . . I forget now whose it was . . . we were home for the day. The sky did not cooperate with our festivities and a steady drizzle of cold rain fell, which made football, basketball, or baseball totally out of the question. Tommy, Billy, and David were at the high school doing something in the gym, which was a fringe benefit of being in high school. Kevin was busy working on a model airplane that had more sticks of balsa wood than a rain forest. When Kev had his eyes on a model plane and his fingers sticky with glue, one didn't attempt to speak to him. He would be at the kitchen table with his creation for the entire day.

Danny, my closest brother, was sick. Really sick. He had

46

gotten sick during the night and spent a goodly part of it either seated on the commode or bending over it, whichever calling was most urgent at the moment. Mama let him move his pain-filled body to the couch and covered him with the quilt from our bed. A small table was moved close to the couch and orange juice was to be kept there for the sick one. Next to the table rested our scrub bucket, mute evidence that Danny was in a very miserable way indeed.

I walked through the two rooms we shared, staying out of the third room, Mama's, because this was off limits except for private conferences which one usually would rather forego. I looked at all the comic books Danny had managed to beg, borrow, or trade. I tried to watch Kevin, but felt his tension mount each time I got close enough to the table to really see what he was doing.

About noon time I left the apartment and went down the street to see if Dickey was home. He was. At least this would be a cure for the oppressive boredom which was filling my young life at the moment.

I wanted to play "Mr. Ree, Detective," but Dickey didn't. He was restless and, I guess, tired of all the games, toys, and things he had in his closet.

"Let's go down to Mason's," he suggested. As usual, the way Dickie said it was more than a suggestion. It was a plain statement of fact. Growing up the youngest of six boys, I had gotten used to taking rather than giving orders. Complying was my middle name. There would be no discussion. We were going to Mason's.

We walked the two blocks to Mason's silently. I kept pulling the collar of my woolen jacket around my neck to keep the soft, cold raindrops from running off my hair and down under the collar. I had forgotten my hat and my black hair caught at least seventy percent of the rain on Hardin Street.

Mason's was an oasis after the walk. The store was warm and smelled of peanuts which roasted just inside the door in a shining monster with a silver door. Naturally, we bypassed the main merchandise area and walked directly to the island of youthful delight—the toy department.

47

It had changed since I had last been in Mason's. Christmas was only a month away and the seasonal toys were there in abundance. I was awestruck by the pressed sawdust pistols in real leather holsters, the shining base metal cars with unchipped paint, the stuffed animals grinning or sticking their felt tongues out at me. Games beyond belief crowded one entire end of the counter: "Sorry," "Parcheesi," and, wonder of all games, "Monopoly" with a metal race car, top hat, flatiron, and other things as playing pieces.

I was standing there looking at the games when I felt Dickey move very close to me and put his hand in my pocket.

"What you doin'?" I asked suddenly.

"Shhhhhhhhhhhh!!" Dickey hissed at me.

I reached in my pocket and felt a flat box about the size of a box of playing cards. I started to pull it out.

"Don't take that out in here!" Dickie whispered urgently.

He scarcely had finished his warning when I felt another presence on my other side. It was Mrs. Hurley, the manager of Mason's! She had moved to me and had her hand firmly on my shoulder.

I looked quickly from her to Dickey but he was nowhere in sight.

"Seán, what do you have in your pocket?" she asked me in a very businesslike tone of voice.

"Nothin'," I started to say, but I knew that there was SOMETHING in there.

Mrs. Hurley reached into my jacket pocket and withdrew a small box. It was a magnet game . . . like those on the counter a few feet away.

"Where did you get this, Seán?" she asked sternly.

"I don't . . . I don't know . . ." was all I could answer.

"You'd better come to the office with me and we'll call your mother," Mrs. Hurley was saying.

I felt like my face was on fire and wished that I had Danny's fever. My ears rang and my vision made everything look like it was miles away. I followed Mrs. Hurley dumbly

48

to the "office."

The office was merely an area of the store which was framed off from the merchandise sector by a low railing. There, a large desk sat and a file cabinet was against the wall.

Mrs. Hurley sat in the chair behind the desk and flatly motioned for me to sit in the chair on the side.

Mama was working and Mrs. Hurley wasn't able to reach her. Kevin, whom she talked to at home, said that he couldn't leave Danny. Mrs. Hurley put the phone in the cradle.

"Seán, I don't like to do this, but stealing is stealing," she said and picked up the phone again. This time she called the police.

I tried to become part of the woodwork. Every customer who passed the "office" looked directly at me and knew that I was a thief. I thought of running, but that thought only lasted for an instant. Having my picture on a poster as a fugitive was more than my mother could bear.

When Pat and Tony walked into the store, all eyes turned to them. They came directly over to us and Mrs. Hurley stepped to the side with them. They talked in quiet tones for a moment and I saw her showing the magnet game to the officers. Then Pat came over to me.

"What did you want this game for, Seán-boy?" Pat asked me in a low tone.

I started to cry and blurted out what I thought was a rational account of what had happened. I told him about Dickey and me coming to Mason's and about my looking at the games and about how I loved to play Monopoly and about how Dickey put his hand in my pocket and about how . . .

I didn't realize it, but I had wet my pants.

Pat went back to Mrs. Hurley and spoke for what seemed a long time. Mrs. Hurley kept throwing stern glances at me as I sat sobbing and wiping my nose on the sleeve of my hand-me-down jacket. She reached over to the desk and grabbed a handful of Kleenex and handed it to me. I tried to mutter a thank you, but started crying harder when she did that.

Pat and Tony came over to me and told me to get up.
I did.

"Let's go out to the car, Seán-boy," Tony said, and I walked between my two captors out into the drizzle. Tony opened the back door of the squad car and I got in. I had never been in a police car before.

The two policemen got in the front seat and Pat turned to me.

"Where's your Mama working today, Seán?" he asked.

"At . . . at . . . at Mrs. Lebowitz's," I managed to get out. My God! They were going to take me to Mrs. Lebowitz's house and Mama and the whole world would know of my caper!

I slid low in the back seat as Pat started the car and drove away from Mason's. We were actually in front of our apartment before I realized where we were. Pat turned to me again.

"O.K., Seán, go on up and change your wet britches." He handed me a huge white handkerchief. "But wipe your nose and eyes first. You don't have to look a mess when your brothers see you!"

I looked at him in amazement.

"Are we going to the police station?" I asked in my trembling voice.

"We are, but you aren't!" Tony laughed.

"We're goin' over to talk a bit with the Hallorans," Pat said. "You stay away from Dickey for a while. He's got a streak about him you don't need to get mixed up in."

"But . . ."

"No 'buts,' Seán. You're too much of a Patrick to steal what you don't have. Get your skinny ass up them steps, now. And—boy-o—don't let me see you with Dickey for a long, long time!"

Tony got out of the car and opened the back door, which, I realized, didn't have an inside door handle. I got out and he put his arm around my shoulder.

"See you on Thursday, Seán," he said.

"Thursday?"

50

"At the bowling alley! You can keep score for us if you want to."

I went upstairs. When I went in, Kevin was standing in the doorway. I guess he had been watching out the window when the police car drove up to let me out.

"Cor, Boy-o, you look a mess! You peed your britches, too!"

I started crying again. Danny was awake and sitting on the couch in his underpants with the quilt wrapped around his shoulders. Kevin sat me down at the table and pushed his model sticks out of the way. I put my head down on my arms and cried for a long time. Kevin stroked my head and neck and Danny sat staring at me but not saying a word.

When I had composed myself, I told them everything that had happened. Kevin was ready to march directly to the Hallorans' house, but I told him that Pat and Tony were going there.

"Change your britches, Seán-o, and wash your face before Mama comes home."

"You gonna tell her?" I asked Kevin and Danny.

"Someday, baby brother," Kevin said. "Someday when it's the right time."

I took my wet pants and underpants off right in the kitchen and Kevin left to take them to the basement, where the soiled clothing was waiting for Mama to wash. I headed to our bedroom to get some clean clothes. Danny stopped me in midstride.

"Come here, Seán-o," he ordered. I went over to my sick brother.

"I don't care if you get what I've got or not," he said, "give your big brother a hug."

I let him hug my neck and felt like I was going to cry again. I didn't, though. I finally got free and got dressed and washed my face. Kevin was back up by the time I got out of the bathroom.

"Feelin' better, Drippy-Britches?" he asked. I told him I was.

"Now, Boy-o, we've got some important work to do," he said.

51

"Work?" I asked.

"Work." Kevin said emphatically. "I've got to teach you how to keep score before Thursday!"

I spent the next hour listening to my brother speak of strikes, spares, and things like that. Danny was back sleeping and the rest of the boys were arriving, pulling off wet jackets and hanging them on the multiple hooks on the kitchen wall, where they steamed in the heat of our crowded room.

Mama came home from Mrs. Lebowitz's and thanked David for putting the potatoes on.

At supper I listened to my brothers tell of their day and the exciting activities they had taken part in.

"What did you do, Seán?" Mama asked.

"Not much, Mama."

Kevin glanced at me with a sideward smile.

Mama let me take Danny's soup and crackers in to him and sit with him while he ate.

The Academicians

OUR SCHOOL, SAINT COLUMBKILLE, was deemed to be one of the finest edifices of academic pursuit in the diocese. Year after year, our teachers would extoll the virtues of learning as practiced by the sisters of Saint Patrick who taught at Saint Columbkille. We were brainwashed with the suggestion that the Publics "didn't hold a candle" to the academic dedication and depth of learning that we were exposed to.

We were also told . . . in absolutely no uncertain terms . . . that the other parochial schools, especially Saint Vitus, where most of the Polish and Ukranian families sent their kids, were trying valiantly but in vain to reach the heights of grandeur so taken for granted at Saint C's.

I still don't know how much truth was to be found in any of the above statements. All I really know is that the Sisters of Saint Patrick were dedicated to the proposition that you were going to learn even if it took physical intervention or years of standing in the "dunce's corner" behind the upright piano.

One of the major, major, major difficulties in being the youngest in a long string of brothers who attended the same school was the fact that your measure was taken the instant you stepped in the classroom. You were categorized, compartmentalized, and judged solely by the behavior of the last Patrick who had been in that class or, if the teacher's memory was good, the behavior of the last several.

"Ah! Mr. Patrick! Seán, is it? Let's see . . . I had Danny last year and Kevin the year before, didn't I? Well, Mr. Patrick, what kind of trouble am I going to have from YOU this year?"

Really, I was fortunate. Danny was a pretty good student and was not a troublemaker. Oh, he had a few scrapes, but didn't even begin to match the reputation fun-loving Kevin had established the year before him. I had fairly comfortable shoes to fill.

53

Unfortunately, my academic prowess was not quite as strong as Danny's, especially in arithmetic. Numbers were, to me, symbols of some ancient culture invented to confound and mystify mankind. Spelling was O.K., and I accepted it as a necessary tool for living, but adding, subtracting, a little multiplying, and simple division were the only skills I thought even remotely useful for a healthy and productive life.

My first day in the sixth grade was my real introduction to following the family in school. Other teachers had mentioned my brothers and, on occasion, referred to an incident or so. My sixth-grade teacher, however, Sister Saint Mary, had been cast from a different mold.

She had had all of the Patrick boys: Tommy, Billy, David, Kevin, and Danny. Now she was to have the youngest. Next year would be the first time in six years that no Patrick would plant his thin bottom on the hard wood of the folding seat on the desk assigned to the family.

Tommy had been a little rambunctious, it appeared, when he entered Sister Saint Mary's class. Billy, unfortunately for the remaining four Patrick boys, was not any better. To put it bluntly, Billy liked to raise hell with teachers, classmates, janitors . . . anyone who happened by. He wasn't mean, cruel, or malicious. He was just a joker and liked to have the last word. It was Billy, in fact, who released in the classroom the sparrow he had caught and yelled "BAT!" at the top of his young lungs.

Forgiveness, for Sister Saint Mary, would cross generations before it materialized.

My sixth-grade year began with omens of ill portent. On my first day I was accosted by Finneran, the janitor, and asked . . . or told . . . to help him carry a heavy lectern to Sister Saint Gabriel's classroom. I did as I was told and, as a result, walked into Sister Saint Mary's classroom five minutes after everyone else. Late on my first day.

"You look like a Patrick," she said with no apparent affection in her voice, "and you're late!"

I began to tell her that Finneran had grabbed me and

made me do some menial work for the betterment of the school, when she stopped me cold.

"Let's get one thing straight, Mister Patrick," she said, pointing a twelve-inch ruler at my pug nose, "I have learned over these many years how to handle you Patricks. Don't think you're going to be an exception in MY classroom."

I didn't think—or want—to be an exception to anything.

"There's the Patrick seat." She motioned to a vacant desk next to "Bloke" Callahan. The Callahans, I was to learn later, also had a seat in Sister Saint Mary's classroom. She had had three of them, two boys and Mary Elizabeth, and still had five more Callahans to go.

I took my appointed seat. The desk top had the name "Patrick" carved in it twice. The carvings were made with an ordinary lead pencil, tracing and retracing the letters an infinity of times. Probably Tommy and Billy, I thought. David, the most sedate and studious of the Patricks, apparently was not even a hazy memory for this Messenger from God to the sixth-grade Irish.

I got through the first day with no real confrontations. We had homework on the first evening, which, in my experience, was unheard of except from Sister Saint Mary. I felt a sigh of relief when the bell rang to send us home.

Outside school I met Danny and Kevin, who were matching baseball cards. I was glad to see them and we started the walk home three abreast.

"You got Mary Mary Quite Contrary, Seán-o?" Kevin asked.

"Yeah. It's gonna be a rough year, I think."

"Bet you got the 'Patrick seat,'" Danny chimed in.

"Right next to Bloke Callahan," I informed him.

"Just don't make waves an' you'll get on O.K. Someone else'll screw up and she'll forget all about you bein' there," Danny said.

I wish it had been that simple. She didn't forget the Patrick seat, even when a Gallagher or an O'Leary took over the class clown's job. In fact, whenever she corrected another male in the classroom she always looked directly at the Patrick seat as if to add, "YOU TOO, PATRICK!" to whatever correction she was dishing out.

After several weeks of taking it on the chin, I felt that if I were going to be treated like a major criminal in that classroom, I might as well have some of the fun the reputation imputed. Inwardly I was afraid to do anything, but my fantasy life grew to fanatical proportions, especially during arithmetic.

I didn't say anything at home about my feelings. When someone would ask how school was going I would tell them it was alright. Even Danny, my closest confidant in the world, had no inkling about my innermost thoughts.

It was Finneran who gave me the idea. Our janitor was an enigma. He was the stuff legends are made of. No one knew where he lived or if he had a family. No one knew where he had come from. He was simply there. He haunted the basement of the annex building where he had his workshop. He serviced the needs of the church, parish house, convent, and school alike. If something was broken it was "get Finneran." Finneran, on his part, would eventually get to the problem in his own good time. One hesitated to encourage faster action because it was suspected that "jogging" Finneran would result in no action at all.

I used to like to help Finneran with the more menial tasks, especially if the helping would get me out of the classroom for a moment of freedom. Often it was simply to help carry a few boxes from the convent to the school or vice-versa. Sometimes, though, it would be to help break apart some furniture or an old crate or something equally exciting.

At these times, I would chatter incessantly and Finneran would respond with grunts and uh-huhs. Occasionally, Finneran would break his vow of silence and tell me to do this or that or, on very rare instances, to ask how Tommy or one of the boys was doing.

I was helping Finneran stack huge piles of school supplies in the annex storeroom one warm afternoon. My experience with Sister Saint Mary that day had been tragic and I was complaining non-stop to the janitor because there was no one else I could complain to.

Finneran went on with his work. I felt that he was miles away from Saint Columbkille at that moment and that he hardly knew I existed except as a pair of skinny arms and a relatively strong back. When I stopped for breath Finneran began talking, as if to himself.

"Oh, Sister Columba, that was a one, she was. My sixth-grade teacher in County Donegal. Mean, she was. The sister of the very divvil, we used to say. Broke a ruler on me one day. Snapped it right in half on my knuckles. Hurt like the divvil!"

He pronounced the Deceiver's name "divvil," but I knew who he meant.

"I did it to her, though, I did, I did . . ." Finneran went on to himself. "Took a thumbtack and, when I got in back of her, tacked her long veil to the chair she was sittin' on. I pressed it in real good. Tricky, it was, but I did it well. When the wench stood up her veil stayed down. Pulled her whole headdress off her evil head, it did!"

I said nothing and Finneran stopped chattering as abruptly as he had started. We continued to stack supplies in piles according to grade. When I had finished and prepared to go, Finneran did an uncharacteristic thing.

He walked me to the door and acknowledged that I had helped him.

"Good job, Seán-boy," he said and then, "Tacked it right to the chair, I did, I did."

With that, he turned away and walked to the basement door where his kingdom lay.

I filed this bit of information in the back of my mind. I continued to help Finneran whenever I was asked for. Nothing further was mentioned about his earlier comments. Then Sister Saint Mary sealed her own doom.

Hazel Giblin had just finished reciting some multiplication table or other. I wasn't really sure because I was busy daydreaming about being allowed to ride Danny's bike after school. When Hazel had finished, Sister Saint Mary must've noted my dreamy expression and called my name . . . twice.

I responded to the second calling with a start. Sister Saint Mary was standing directly over me and loomed like an avenging angel of death.

"All you Patricks are the same!" she shouted to the world and to our class. "You're a bunch of dreamers and you'll never amount to anything . . . none of you!"

My face turned crimson. I felt the blush to the roots of my black hair. I am positive that steam must have come from my ears.

". . . like your brothers, a troublemaker!" she was hollering, on a roll. I sat there and said nothing. You NEVER talked back to a nun.

When she had finished her tirade, she strode back to her desk and, after a few moments of caustic glances in my direction and a visible effort to calm herself, went on with the lesson. She ignored me for the rest of the day but my mortification was complete.

"Jeez, Seán!" Bloke whispered, "the bitch got all over you, didn't she?"

I didn't answer. But my plan formed of its own accord in my Irish noggin. Visions of thumbtacks filled my brain and arithmetic filtered out. This rather shy, relatively passive, and thoroughly embarrassed Patrick began to plot.

This moment of infamy had fallen on a Friday afternoon. I had the whole weekend to polish my plan. On Monday morning I would be ready.

I was awake before Mama even called us on Monday. I was out of bed like a shot and pulled on my corduroys and knit shirt before Danny had stirred from his pillow. Breakfast was a tossed-down affair. I waited impatiently for Kev and Danny to get their books and lunches.

"C'mon, you guys, we'll be late!"

"Hold your butt on, Seán-o! We got plenty of time!" Kev shouted at me.

I had my books, my lunch and, in my pocket, carefully wrapped in a piece of paper, my weapon of revenge. It was a silver thumbtack secretly removed from a corner of the kitchen shelf where it had held the flowered shelf paper for a number of years.

I really didn't hear much during that class. The students functioned without me. I waited for my opportunity. I knew it would come, because I firmly believed in a just God watching over me. It finally came after lunch.

"You, McDermott . . . you, Killkenny . . . you, Patrick . . . you, Lynch . . . go to the board and write the next four problems."

"The board" was directly in back of Sister Saint Mary's desk. I would be in the position I had waited for so patiently since eight thirty that morning. I whispered to Bloke.

"Ask her a question, Bloke!" I hissed.

"What?" Bloke said in a puzzled tone.

"Ask her a damn question!"

I walked to my position in back of her desk. Her long veil was draped over the back of her chair and hung well below the seat of her sturdy, wooden chair.

My invective must have shown Bloke how important this matter was to me. "S'ter!" Bloke called out, raising his hand.

"What do YOU want, Mr. Callahan?" Sister answered.

Bloke began asking her some dumb question about the Bible or something. I didn't hear the question. I dropped my chalk.

I bent to retrieve it. In so doing, I took the tack which was already in my hand and pinned it solidly into the chair . . . after sticking it through the veil first. I rose and casually "bumped" Sister's chair so that any movement on my part would have a reason.

"Ooooops! Dropped my chalk, S'ter . . ." I muttered.

"Pick it up, Mr. Patrick. Don't just look at it like a dunce."

The class sniggered.

We finished our problems on the board and returned to our seats. Four more victims advanced to the board and Sister continued to involve herself at her desk while they did the next four problems. Sister usually waited until the entire exercise was on the board before she rose and found thirty thousand faults with our attempts at arithmetic.

"What did you do, Seán-o?" Bloke asked me under his breath.

"Hold on!" was all I answered.

The last group of four finished with their board time and returned to their seats. Sister Saint Mary turned her head and glanced at the work. She turned back to the class.

"Now we'll see just how little you've actually learned," she said and began to rise from her chair.

I held my breath.

She rose to her majestic height . . . almost. She started out of her chair and then it happened. Her head was abruptly snapped back and her starched bonnet began to leave its moorings!

"Wha...........!" she started to say. It was too late for her to sit back down. Her balance was already thrown backwards.

Her veil didn't come completely off. It held halfway back on her head. But Sister Saint Mary was off balance. She, veil, and chair all continued to move backwards. It was slow motion . . . it was ballet . . . it was wonderful!

Back, back, back she went and she and the chair tumbled on the floor. The clatter sounded like cannon fire! The sight was glorious!

Three or four girls ran forward to help the hapless torturer of young Irish boys. She was lifted, the tack discovered, and the damage undone. But it was sufficient.

I had had my revenge.

Later that week Finneran again asked for my help in the annex. We were to break up a crate that some fixtures had come in.

"Yeah, pulled her headdress right off, it did! We did laugh, though! It's not nice to fool with a nun but, Cor! This 'un deserved it. The very Wrath of God she was . . ."

And, when I listened carefully, I detected a subtle laughter which Finneran attempted to hide.

He couldn't hide his eyes, though.

". . . never found out who did it, she didn't," he went on. "Never found out. But I knew . . . and that was enough.

"Seán-boy! Let's get this crate apart. We ain't got all day now, do we, boy-o?"

"Right to it, Mr. Finneran!" I grinned as I answered. "Yes, sir!"

Kaddish for Mr. Feldman

ALTHOUGH WE WERE MOSTLY an Irish Catholic neighborhood, we had a smattering of Italians, Polish, and Jews. We intermixed freely because we all had poverty in common. We were a neighborhood and, as such, an entity to ourselves.

Mr. Feldman was a very important part of my neighborhood. We had always been instructed by Mama to be polite to all older people and to show respect for them, regardless of whether they had different backgrounds than we had.

Mr. Feldman and his wife lived on the floor below us in the three-story apartment building which was my home from birth until my entry into the navy at age nineteen.

They were very old for as long as I can remember. Mrs. Feldman was a short, rather plump lady with the whitest hair I can ever recall seeing. Her husband was tall and always wore a hat. Mama said that Jews—at least male Jews—always covered their heads out of respect for God. This impressed me, as we Catholics always made sure that our stocking hats were removed upon entry into our church.

Mr. and Mrs. Feldman were retired from some business they had operated for many years. They were always seen together and they looked for all the world like Mutt and Jeff as they walked home from their short trips to the neighboring stores. I always said a polite hello to them and they responded with a nod and, sometimes, even a mention of my name.

"Hello, Seán," Mr. Feldman would say, "and how is your mother today?"

Always the same thing.

One day, shortly before my thirteenth birthday, I helped Mr. Feldman carry a couple of bags of groceries to his apartment. Mrs. Feldman had not been feeling well, and Mr. Feldman had done the meager shopping for the two of them.

Our conversation was not anything earthshaking. We spoke of the weather and about the neighborhood . . . and about school. Adults always ask about school. When we reached the Feldmans' door, Mr. Feldman reached up with his fingers and stroked a small tube attached to the frame of the door at about shoulder height. He touched the fingers to his lips and then opened the door. I followed him into a clean apartment and set the bag I was carrying on the kitchen table.

"What did you do that for?" I asked him.

"What for?" he responded.

"That thing you did at the door." I was always inquisitive.

"Oh . . . the *mazuzah*. . . ." He led me back to the door.

"This little tube contains a very tiny paper and it has sacred words written on it. I touch it and kiss my fingers to show respect for God's words to us."

"What does it say?" I pestered.

"It is from our Torah . . . your Bible. It begins, 'Hear, O Israel, the Lord our God, the Lord is One . . .' and then goes on."

This was my introduction to Judaism.

Mr. and Mrs. Feldman liked me and soon began to ask me to do things for them on occasion. I never minded and Mama insisted that I refuse the nickel that Mr. Feldman invariably offered.

"They need their nickels more than you do," Mama said.

As our relationship grew, I felt freer to ask Mr. Feldman about things that I had heard about Jews.

"We don't eat pork or shellfish," he explained, "because it is forbidden in our Torah."

On certain occasions, Mrs. Feldman would insist that I stay and share their meal. On those times she would bring a set of dishes out of a cupboard and explain that these were dishes that a "goy" could eat off of. She even explained that they would be washed separately from her other dishes. I didn't feel offended, though, because I figured that this was just a part of their religion and we had some pretty strange practices, too.

The Feldmans had a son whose name was Jerry. He was away in college and seldom came home. When he did, it was an occasion for feasting and I was often invited. I remember being a guest at one Passover meal and hearing Jerry, then about twenty years old, ask the ageless question, "Father, why is this night different from all other nights?"

As I let my mind drift back to those times, I recall two incidents with a clarity that amazes me, even to this day.

Jerry Feldman had joined the marines. Korea was a place we had heard of, but we had no idea where it was. Early in the conflict, the Feldmans were informed that their only son, Jerry, had given his life for his country. This was in the spring of 1952 when I was fourteen.

"I know, Mrs. Patrick, that it is unusual," Mr. Feldman told Mama, "but I would so much appreciate it if you would join me . . . all of you . . . and Mrs. Feldman to share our Passover this year."

Naturally, Mama said yes.

We gathered around the table laden with things that none of my brothers had seen before. There was the bitter herb, the chopped eggs and livers, the glasses of sweet wine . . .

"Seán," Mr. Feldman said, "You are the youngest male present . . . ."

He handed me a small paper with questions written on it.

"Will you honor my house?"

"Why is this night different from all other nights?" I began.

I felt that I could sense the passage of the angel's wings that night as I took the place of a young Jew who had fallen in the honored glory which knows no nationality, nor religion, nor prejudice . . . .

We ate standing in the ageless tradition of the Passover. We shared the cup and we dipped our bitter herbs, Mama and her six very Irish sons.

In the glow from the seven candles in the *menorah* I could see the tears in the eyes of the Feldmans, and in Mama's eyes, too.

For the years we lived in the same apartment, I would continue to help the Feldmans when they needed me. My brother Danny and I lifted and carried and shared with them.

Mrs. Feldman was a true "Jewish mother," and her chicken soup brought many a Patrick from the brink of death when colds or flu attacked.

Mr. Feldman died on my first furlough from the navy. He had been ill for a while and Mama and Danny, who was in college, assisted Mrs. Feldman when and where they could.

I was home for thirty days and was preparing for my assignment to the Gulf of Iran when Mr. Feldman turned for the worse.

"He's going, Seán," Mrs. Feldman told me as I entered the small bedroom. Mr. Feldman lay propped up on pillows and I was gratified to see that he had a small skullcap on his head in spite of his illness.

I advanced towards the bed. Mr. Feldman recognized me and held out a feeble hand. I took it in mine and felt an unexplainable warmth towards this man who was about to enter God's kingdom.

"Seán," was all he could say. He had difficulty breathing and Mama, who was standing on the side of the bed with her arms around Mrs. Feldman, indicated that I should just stay and let him hold my hand.

"Seán," he said again after a few minutes, "I would be honored if you would say *Kaddish* for me . . . ."

I looked puzzled and Mrs. Feldman gestured that she would explain. I held tightly to Mr. Feldman's hand and looked at him, hoping that he could see me.

"I will say *Kaddish* for you," I told him, not even knowing what *Kaddish* was. He smiled and held his other hand out. Mrs. Feldman took it in hers.

He died that way.

Later that same day, because the Jews do not observe the "wake" like the Irish and usually bury their dead before sundown, I arrived at the synagogue. We were all there—

65

Tommy, who was now a lawyer; Billy, a fireman; David, who was home for Easter from his graduate studies at Notre Dame; Kevin, also a fireman; Danny, who was an accountant; and me . . . the sailor.

A man handed each of us a black skullcap. When I reached for mine, he said that I should just keep my navy cap on.

We stood there wondering what to do when a bearded man came over to us and we entered the temple. Mrs. Feldman had spoken to him and he gestured to me.

"Please come with me," he said, and led me to the front of the small congregation.

I stood that day with other Jewish males who made up the required number necessary for *Kaddish*. I didn't understand all of what was said because most of it was in Hebrew. But I knew that my Irish Catholic prayers were acceptable to God, anyway.

At the conclusion of the service I couldn't help myself. I needed to lift my voice one last time for a friend.

"Hear, O Israel," I began, "the Lord our God, the Lord is One!"

A bearded man who was wearing a prayer shawl reached his arm up and put it around my shoulders and I continued my prayer, oblivious to those in the synagogue. My brogue was pronounced but I felt that God didn't really care if His words were spoken with a brogue or with a Yiddish accent.

"You will love the Lord, your God, with all of your heart, with all of your soul, and with all of your strength. You will love your neighbor as yourself . . ."

The words in the *mazuzah*. I didn't see anything Catholic or Jewish in those words. They were for all of us. I did see Mr. Feldman in them. And I prayed for his safe passage to Glory and for the expectation of seeing him again when I, too, would make that passage.

Mama came up to me and put her hand on me. I wept silently as I stood there in my blue uniform.

In my mind, I pictured a fourteen-year-old Irish boy, surrounded by his brothers, raising the millenium-old question at the Passover table.

"Why is this night different from all other nights?"

I could hear the crack as the wizened hands broke the ceremonial *matzohs* to hand to each of us. I could feel the fringe of the tassels on his prayer shawl brush against my bare arm as he stood beside me at the table.

"Because, my son, on this night God delivered His people . . ."

And I knew that God had, indeed, delivered Mr. Feldman because he loved Him . . . and us . . . very much.

Smoker's Cough

IF THERE WAS ANYTHING Mama considered a dirty habit, it was smoking. She had little patience with people who rushed out of church at the end of Mass on Sunday to light up a Camel or a Chesterfield. She had less patience when one of my brothers would even intimate that he was considering starting the practice.

No one in our household smoked. My Uncle Jerry did, but wisely refrained when he came to our apartment to visit. It was less bother to sit for a while visiting smokelessly than to light up and risk the lecture which was sure to follow when Mama noticed the blue smoke curling at her kitchen table.

One morning, at breakfast, Tommy tried to be a wise guy and almost ruined the meal for the rest of the family.

I wasn't paying attention to any of the morning conversation. I was too engrossed feeling in the Rice Krispies box for the prize promised on the back and had my arm up to the elbow in the cereal. Danny was waiting patiently for me to find the prize.

"I think I'll go out in the hall for a quick smoke before school," Tommy said loudly enough for Mama, standing by the stove, to hear.

"Thomas!" The shout made me almost drop the box of cereal. Then the lecture on the evils of smoking began—the filth, the expense, the horrible damage to heart, lungs, kidneys, and various and assorted organs. . . .

"Mama! I was only kidding!" Tommy tried to explain. But it was too late.

Kevin tried to change the subject.

"Mama! Seán's got his whole arm in the Rice Krispies and he picks his nose!"

No response. I could have poured the box of crackly morsels on Kevin's head and it would have been unnoticed except by Kevin and me.

Mama always ended her lectures on smoking with making each of us take a solemn pledge to refrain from tobacco for life and afterlife.

That breakfast was no fun at all. Tommy genuinely earned the looks of derision shot at him from all directions.

I really never gave smoking too much thought. It was something which didn't bother me one way or the other. On the rare occasions when I'd be exposed to it, I noticed that my eyes burned a bit and that the smell was not too inviting, but that was all. I actually enjoyed the smell of cigar smoke and vowed that, should I ever consider smoking, it would be cigars.

One day, though, I was taking a load of laundry to Mrs. Weiss's house for Mama. Mr. Weiss smoked cigars. I was told to wait in the den for Mrs. Weiss to get Mama's money. Mr. Weiss had extinguished a cigar there earlier. The smell of a dead, cold cigar was certainly anything but inviting, and at that point I vowed that I would NOT smoke cigars, either.

Danny and I hung around with Dale O'Leary and Ritchie Saperstein. Ritchie was one of the only Jewish kids in the neighborhood who came from as abject poverty as we Irish, and that made him one of us. Dale, on the other hand, came from a financially stable family. His father was an accountant for the Natural Gas Company and made a regular and substantial living.

One Sunday morning after the Kids' Mass we ran into Ritchie and Dale, who were heading for the local park. The "park" wasn't really much more than a couple of lots which belonged to the city and which still had several trees on them. We used to go there to play mumblety-peg with our pen knives or, when we were younger, to swing on the three swings which hung on heavy chains from great heights.

Danny was Dale's best friend at the time and sat next to him in Sister Saint Gabriel's classroom. It was only natural that Danny would want to know where Dale and Ritchie were going and what they were going to do.

"Just goin' to the park, Dan-o. Maybe smoke a stick of

tobacco or two. . . ."

Danny was a little shocked. I could see it on his face. I was shocked, too, but didn't dare say anything because I was "the kid" and my opinion was valueless.

"Cor! You guys are smokin' in the park?"

Ritchie produced a package of Spud cigarettes from his pants pocket. He carried them right in his pocket! That, to me, was an unnecessary risk. I once had a matchbook with a drawing of a scantily clad lady on it, but would never have dreamed of keeping it where it could be found by another human being. I kept it hidden in a hole in a brick in the basement wall of the apartment. The moisture eventually got to it, though, and it mushed.

"You comin' with us?" Dale asked Danny.

"I don't know." Danny hesitated. "Me and Seán have got to get home and change."

But I could tell he was hooked.

"Can Squirt keep his gob shut?" Dale asked Danny. I riled at being called "Squirt"—especially by Dale.

"He's O.K.," said Danny. He could have been a little more defensive of me, I thought, but I was twelve at the time and not very aggressive.

"I still don't know . . ." said Danny. But he was weakening. I could tell what Danny was thinking.

"We'll only be a little while," Dale said. That seemed to clinch it.

"C'mon, Seán-o . . ." Danny said to me, "an' keep your trap shut about this!"

We walked the short block to the park and went deep into the "woods," which was simply a fairly thick grove of trees. Almost dead center in the "woods" was a small clearing large enough for the four of us to squat without leaning on each other.

Ritchie took out the pack of Spuds again. Dale, on his part, furnished each of us with a half-stick of Beeman's Pepsin Chewing Gum, which he told us to chew after smoking the tobacco. It would, he said, make the odor of tobacco on our breath virtually undetectable.

Ritchie lit his cigarette first. He struck a light with a wooden kitchen match he also carried in his pocket. As he held the flame to the tip of the cigarette I could see the end glow to life. He moved the flaming stick away from the paper tube of tobacco and let a cloud of smoke escape from his lips. It seemed that the clearing was suddenly cloudy and misty.

"Give me some fire, too, Ritchie," Dale commanded. He, too, had a cigarette in his lips and reached out for the still flaming match Ritchie was holding.

Dale did exactly as Ritchie had done and smoke encircled his head. I noticed, for the first time, that smoke also came out of his nose!

"Have a fag!" Ritchie said to Danny, holding the Spuds out to him. I watched my brother carefully.

Danny reached out and took the package from Ritchie. He slowly removed a cigarette and looked at it. It had a cork tip.

He put the cigarette to his lips and Dale lit a second match. This he held for Danny and my brother leaned forward to let the flame kiss the end of the cigarette.

"Draw in, Danny," Dale urged.

Danny "drew in."

I could see the cigarette catch the flame. It actually looked like the flame leaped forward to the cigarette when Danny inhaled.

Danny coughed and then coughed again. It wasn't much of a spasm but it made me jump.

"C'mon, Squirt," Ritchie urged, offering me the pack of Spuds, "Have a smoke. It'll put hair on your chest!"

I wasn't particularly interested in a hairy chest at the time. Body hair was not what was concerning me. It was the fact that I was being offered a cigarette. For some reason, the whole thing scared me.

"Go 'head, Seán-o," Danny said, "I won't tell."

I took the cigarette. It was extraordinarily light. I had expected it to be heavier. I put the thing to my lips.

The cork tip was pure window dressing in those days.

71

Filters hadn't been invented and I immediately got a few specks of tobacco in my mouth. I tried to spit them out.

"Quit spittin', Seán!" Dale commanded.

He lit another match and put it to my cigarette. I remembered his admonishment to Danny to "draw in," and so I "drew in."

In an instant I felt the hot smoke flood my mouth. I instinctively gasped and the smoke poured into my throat. I began coughing violently.

Danny reached over and slapped my back. Dale and Ritchie were much less understanding. Ritchie gave me a disgusted look and Dale was openly sarcastic.

"I told you that he was too young!"

He did NOT tell anyone I was too young. He was only a year older than I was, anyway.

I stopped coughing finally and leaned back against a tree. The other three continued to smoke and to extol the virtues of tobacco.

Danny didn't have much to add to anything the other two were saying, but he would nod knowingly from time to time.

Ritchie, especially, seemed to be the most knowledgeable about the matter. He told of smoking Camels "when I can get 'em." Camels were the cigarettes endorsed by Buster Crabbe.

I sat there looking at this thing held between my index and middle fingers. I had seen how to hold cigarettes at the movies. This was the way—apparently—it was done. The smoke curled up from the tip and even exited the cork end slightly. I puffed occasionally, but very shallowly so that I would not begin coughing again and have to endure the wrath of Dale and Ritchie.

Danny was doing about the same as I was. I watched him. He was only taking an occasional "drag" from the cigarette and it was easy to see that he held the smoke solidly in his mouth, not letting any find its disastrous path to his esophagus.

Ritchie and Dale lit a second cigarette. Danny said he was

"fine," and I was not consulted.

None of us heard any footsteps. We were not paying attention, anyway. But suddenly a figure loomed over us. "WHAT DO YOU THINK YOU ARE DOING?" thundered out directly over my head. I must have jumped at least five feet straight in the air! I was so surprised that I actually rolled over on my side from my cross-legged position!

"WHAT ARE YOU DOING, RICHARD?" It was Mr. Saperstein. He stood there, six feet of him, in his black trousers and collarless white shirt. His head, as always, was covered by a brushed black Homburg hat.

If I wanted to exaggerate, I would say that Ritchie attempted to swallow the cigarette. He didn't, but I'm sure that the action was at least in his mind for a moment.

Danny was the only one who jumped up. He rose like a cat jumping back from a hot candle. His fair Irish complexion was death white. Our family freckles stood out like pendots on his face.

Mr. Saperstein was not discriminatory. He grabbed my shirt with one hand and literally lifted me to my feet. With his other hand, he had Ritchie by the scruff of his neck and propelled him to a standing position. Dale and Danny were too frozen to move. In later years, I would compare our expressions with that of Mike Moriarty when he peed on the electric fence at summer camp.

"SO! SMOKING! SO!" Mr. Saperstein might as well have held a bullhorn. The WORLD would now know of our dastardly deed.

"You want to smoke? I'll give you smoke . . . right on the seat of your pants."

Ritchie started to say something. I don't know what he was going to say, but it was cut off at its inception by Mr. Saperstein's huge hand landing a clean SLAP! on Ritchie's posterior.

"Come now!" he commanded. "Let's show your mamas what big, grown-up boys they have!"

We were marched, in front of Mr. Saperstein, the two

blocks to our apartment. Dale and Ritchie were ordered to stay on the stoop and WAIT until Mr. Saperstein had delivered Danny and me to our fate.

Mama was surprised when David let us—and Mr. Saperstein—in the kitchen door. She stood with her hands on her hips while he explained our transgression. I stood close to Danny and watched the pot of potatoes steaming as they boiled on the stove. I could feel the heat of embarrassment and shame radiating from my brother's body. Or was it from mine?

Mama thanked Mr. Saperstein for finding, stopping, and delivering us. Before he left, he shook his finger seven thousand times in Danny's and my faces.

"Don't you EVEREVEREVEREVER let me catch you fooling around like that again! You HEAR? You HEAR? Next time I come with Officer Shaugnessy!"

He turned and went down the stairs with the dignity of DeGaulle.

After Mr. Saperstein had gone, Mama turned to us.

"You two should get a whippin'," she began. Her tone was not loud. It was soft and tired. "But you're gettin' too big for the hairbrush. You know what I think of smokin' and there's no sense my repeatin' myself all over again."

She paused and looked us directly in the eyes.

"Is it that you'll be wantin'? Smokin'?"

We both shook our heads "no." Danny started to say something about getting even with Dale and Ritchie, but Mama cut him off with a look.

"You'll be doin' nothing like that. Did they hold that divvil cigarette to your thin lips? Did they breathe in the smoke for ye?"

She had a point.

We were not allowed to listen to "Inner Sanctum" that week, nor were we allowed to go to the movies on Saturday afternoon. But that was the extent of our punishment.

Our brothers were informed of our experiment at the Sunday dinner table. Mama always roasted three chickens from the live poulterers where David worked. He was instructed to buy one on Saturday and Mr. Schmidt would

74

give him two others for the family as a bonus for a good week's work.

As the platters were passed, Mama told of Mr. Saperstein's visit again for those who were not in the kitchen when he came by with us. We were looked at, stared at, and subjected to silent headshakes from our seniors.

Then, as if by agreement, nothing more was said.

Being the youngest, Danny and I went to bed a half-hour before the rest of the boys. We hung our clothes on the hooks on the wall and brushed our teeth with Dr. Lyons' Toothpowder and salt.

I got in first because I slept on the half of the bed against the wall. Danny slid in next to me.

"Danny?"

"What, Seán-o?" Danny would never, ever call me Squirt.

"Did ye like it? The cigarette?"

"Cor! Baby brother! No, I didn't. The damned thing made me want to cough me lungs out!"

I had never heard Danny swear before but I thought that God, in His Heaven, would be tolerant under the circumstances.

"I didn't like it either, Danny."

It was dark in our room and I could barely see the outline of Danny's face when I turned to him.

"Danny?"

"What, Seán-o? It's time for sleepin'."

I didn't like to make Danny impatient with me, but I was curious.

"Danny, you gonna clobber Dale and Ritchie?"

Danny was silent for a moment. Then he reached around me and put his arm around my shoulders. I rested my neck in the crook of my favorite brother's elbow.

"Naw, Seán-o . . . I'm gonna let them cigarettes get 'em!"

I laughed and rubbed my nose on Danny's cheek. He pulled his arm free of my shoulders and popped me easily on the right arm. It didn't hurt, though.

75

The Sweater

"THE SWEATER" CAME INTO our family when I was just a little more than eight years old. Tommy, my oldest brother, was fourteen and was the first to wear it. I was about that age, too, when it came to be my turn to have it as my very own. In between, Billy had his turn, as well as David, Kevin, and Danny, too.

This particular sweater was a gift to all of us from Uncle Michael, Mama's brother. He had taken a vacation trip back to Ireland and spent a bit of time visiting some of the far-flung O'Hickeys who made up Mama's family. One branch lived on the island of Inishmaan, which is the second of the three Aran Isles.

Apparently, not much goes on out on those desolate islands. The islanders fish, do a little farming, and raise a few sheep, but that's about it. I have seen pictures of these islands and they surely appear to be at the very end of the earth.

Anyway, let me get back to this sweater.

Uncle Michael had spent a goodly amount of time in Ireland and returned full of stories and tales about the family. Mama was anxious for his visit to our apartment after his return. Since he was a bachelor he was, as Mama put it, kind of hard to keep up with.

On the first Sunday after his return to the United States, Uncle Michael was invited to share our usual chicken dinner. He accepted and arrived shortly after our return from Mass at St. Columbkille Church. He looked happy, ruddy, and full of the very "divvil" as he literally bounced through our door and swung Mama around in a brotherly embrace. Under his arm he carried a thick paper-wrapped parcel which was tied with string.

Mama broke free from Uncle Michael's exuberance and started back to the stove, but Uncle Michael halted her in mid-step.

"Hold, Katy!" he laughed. "These buckos need to see what I've got tucked under me arm and I want you to see it, too."

We gathered around him and he handed Tommy the brown paper parcel.

"Here, Tom. Since you're the eldest of the Patricks this goes to you first. It may not seem like much, but I'm sure that each of you will find it special in your own time."

Tommy looked to Mama to see if it was alright for him to open the parcel. She nodded and we all bent forward to see what it was.

"Cor!" Tommy exclaimed as he carefully removed the rustling paper from the soft object inside.

There, folded carefully and springing to fluffy life as the restraining paper was removed, was the whitest and most beautiful sweater I have ever seen. The soft wool was fuzzy with newness and the strands which made it were as thick as pencils. Tommy lovingly unfolded the sweater and held it for all of us to see.

It was beautiful. It was unique. It was so different. The sweater was white but seemed to shimmer with a glow all its own. The maker had knitted an intricate pattern of scrollwork reminiscent of the Celtic designs we had seen in pictures. On the front we could see the complicated scrolls intertwining and circling each other. We were breathless.

"Cor!" we all exclaimed in awe.

"It's beautiful, Michael!" Mama said in a very soft and hushed voice. "It's Aran, that's to be seen at a glance."

"Aye. It's Aran. I got it on Inishmaan from Uncle Neeley. Wouldn't take a cent for it, either. He told me it was for Kate's boys and theirs after."

"It is the O'Hickey, then?"

"'Tis the O'Hickey," Uncle Michael said. We looked slightly left out.

"Boys," Mama explained, "look well at the sweater because you've never seen one like it. The sweater is Aran and it's from me family. It's an O'Hickey sweater."

Between Uncle Michael and Mama we learned that the

seafaring life on the Aran Isles was difficult indeed. It was not uncommon for a fisherman to set out on a calm sea and be confronted by a violent change in weather. Some of these fishermen never returned alive to their island homes.

Wool was plentiful on the Arans because sheep were the only animals raised in any numbers. The wool was carefully carded and spun and the Aran women knitted this into garments to shield them from the cold. Each family had its pattern and that pattern was carefully knitted into the heavy white sweaters such as the one Tommy now pulled over his blue shirt.

"Cor! It feels so soft and good!" he exclaimed as he stood proudly wearing the huge, bulky garment which sagged a bit on his slim frame.

"The reason, boys, that each family has its own pattern is so that if a man is lost at sea it will be possible to identify him when he is picked up or washed ashore many weeks later. The sea isn't kind and often a person cannot be recognized by his face anymore."

"But they can tell by the sweater!" David almost shouted.

"Aye. They can. It's the family mark and the mark claims the man as one of their own."

"But we're Patricks!" said my next oldest brother, Danny.

"You're from O'Hickey stock, too!" Mama said. "You've the right to wear the O'Hickey pattern and wear it proudly."

"Tom," Uncle Michael said, "you're the first. After you Billy will wear it and then right down the line to young Seán."

"You better take care of it for me!" I butted in.

"No need to worry, Seán-o," Uncle Michael said. "This sweater will outlast all of you and many of yours will wear it, too."

"May it carry the luck o' the Irish!" Mama concluded.

The sweater did make the rounds. Tommy wore it for a year and then it was Billy's turn . . . and so on. When it got to me it still looked like new. I guess it was worn, somewhat, but not noticeably. It was cared for like no other article of clothing in our family and, as it came the next Patrick's turn to possess the sweater, it was passed with an air of ceremony and solemnity from the current wearer's hands to those of the next one.

I remember the day the sweater came to me. I had just turned fifteen and waited impatiently for Danny to finish his turn. Finally, at supper on a Wednesday night, Danny excused himself from the table and came back carrying the sweater over his arm. Billy, David, Kevin, and Mama were all there. Only Tommy, in Korea with the United States Navy, was absent. Danny held the sweater out to me and said, "It's yours now, Seán-o."

"Is it really my turn?" I asked, a little surprised at the emotion which welled up in me.

"It is," he said. "I've had it long enough and it's time for you to wear the mark."

Mama came over to me and kissed my cheek. I held the soft wool close to me and felt its warmth, its friendliness, and its protection. It was actually, really, the very first time I had held the sweater.

My brothers smiled at me. That night each would give me a hug or a kiss in his own turn and his own time. I knew it was the congratulations for my "passage" and I truly felt that I had entered an entire new era in my life.

So strange for a sweater to bring such feelings. . . . I wore it that night. I went outside and walked to St. Columbkille Church so that everyone would see that I was the Patrick with the sweater now. Probably no one even noticed, but I felt that all eyes were on me. Father O'Phelan was sitting on the large porch of the rectory.

"So, Seán-o, it's come to you now?" He had noticed!

"How did you know, Father?" I asked him.

"I've family in the Arans, too. I'd know a sweater from there like I know me own hand. Besides, I've known about your family sweater since your Uncle Michael gave it to Tommy."

"Did Tommy tell you all about our sweater?"

"Aye, Seán-o. He told me all about it and how it was to

79

pass from him on to the rest of you. He wore it here right after your Uncle gave it to him and we prayed that evening."

"I didn't know that."

"Not only him, but after him Billy and then David. Kevin came then and last year Danny was the one. Strange how you all end up here after the passin' of the sweater."

"Maybe there's somethin' in the sweater that brings us here."

Father O'Phelan had gotten out of his chair and guided me across the walkway towards the massive church. He was talking as we walked into a side door and entered the cool and very dark house of God.

"I've always had a prayer, Seán-o, that, like the women in the Arans who put their identity into the wool they knit—to identify their own—God would knit me a sweater to wear with His own mark on it. Then, if something happened to me, everyone would know that I belonged to Him."

"That's nice, Father."

We knelt at the altar rail and Father said a very special prayer for the wearer of the O'Hickey—now the Patrick—sweater. He prayed that we would be protected from harm and that we would always bring honor to the family who was identified by the design in the wool. He prayed, finally, that God would knit "a sweater with His own mark on it so that this young wearer may be called Yours and that all may know to whom he belongs."

The sweater has crossed generations but it is still in our family. My daughter is the one who has it now. It is showing the wear a bit, but the pattern is still clear and the wool is still soft.

"Thanks, Dan-o," I said as I nudged my brother that night in our bed.

"It's time that you wear it, brother," Danny said to me.

"Danny?"

"What, Seán-o?"

"Did it make ya feel special? Did you feel kind of different when you put it on?"

"I did, Seán-o. I felt kind of special and grown up."

"So did I, just when I put it on. I felt like it belonged on me."

"It does, Seán-o."

"Did Father O'Phelan tell you about God's sweater?"

"He did."

"I prayed that God would knit me a sweater, too, Dan-o."

"I know."

"I prayed He would knit one for each of us . . . 'specially for you."

"Thanks, brother."

The Gimp

LOOKING BACK I SHOULD consider our family especially blest healthwise. Most of us survived the ordinary and common childhood diseases with no ill effects. Actually, when one of us got something, a conscious effort was made to expose the whole batch to the dread malady so that we would all get it over at one time.

In our childhood days, many diseases such as Measles, Chicken Pox, Mumps, Scarlet Fever, and Whooping Cough all had a mandatory quarantine period for the entire household. I remember vividly when David had the measles. The public health nurse came to the house and examined him. When what she had suspected was verified, the hammer came out and the orange sign was posted on the front and back doors of our apartment indicating that dread sickness dwelt within.

Colds were indeed common. If someone were not sniffling we considered it a rare day. But colds were not thought to be incapacitating and life went on.

The most serious mishap was the one which happened to Danny, my next older brother.

Like the rest of us, Danny had suffered the scrapes and sprains of a boy growing up. Sports took an active toll on our bodies, but usually nothing that a little Sloan's Liniment or a Band-Aid wouldn't cure.

Danny was an outgoing kid. He's still very outgoing, but when he was a kid he was a comedian and a showman. Like Tommy, Danny was quick-witted and could usually come out on top of any argument, could top the joke someone else told, and was really the "life of the party." Danny gravitated to center stage at the drop of a hat. He was well liked and popular, the envy of his younger brother.

This led to a related problem. Danny hated to be left out and could not stand being uninformed. Curiosity was his undoing.

As I have mentioned, when Danny was fourteen and I thirteen we worked on Patrick's Corner, Danny hawking the evening news and I shining shoes. I loved being on Patrick's Corner with Danny because it was fun being identified with him. People bought their papers from Danny because they liked him. They got their shoes shined by me because I was Danny's brother. (And because I did a really good job . . . after awhile!)

Danny had a businessman's sense. He soon knew the names of his regular customers and always tossed in a friendly "'Evenin', Mr. Flaherty!" with the paper. He knew which customers preferred their papers folded and which ones wanted them "flat open" so that they could immediately scan the front page.

"You just watch 'em, Seán," he told me one day. "If they fold it and stick it under their arm for two days they're a foldie. If they usually look at the front page while they're walkin' away they're flats."

As much as I envied Danny's job as "hawker," I feared the day I would advance to that position because I knew that Danny's shoes were big to fill when it came to meeting and serving people successfully. It took me a long enough time to establish myself as the Shoeshine Patrick and, for several months, I was referred to as "the new one" by the regulars. My work was invariably compared to Danny's shines. In time I became my own person, but only after a lengthy apprenticeship.

Danny and I looked like Patricks. All of us resembled each other. But Danny and I were so very much alike that there was no mistaking the relationship. Black hair, pug noses, and millions of freckles which would not disappear until long after adulthood had set in. Even David, who was the only redhead in the family, had enough of the rest of the family traits to be immediately identified as one of us. When people referred to one of us it was usually collective. I used to think that we lacked individual identity . . . but it really didn't matter.

My brother, Danny, was also my closest confidant. I

shared a lot with Kevin and, when I really needed a serious shoulder to cry on or to lean on, went to him. But my deepest thoughts and my most personal dreams were shared with Danny. At night, in bed before the older boys came in for their sleep, I used to talk quietly with Danny and, here, get the advice, encouragement, or admonition that I needed.

I took advice from Danny, too. I always carefully considered what he told me because—in spite of his fun-loving, joking spirit—he would not steer his baby brother wrong.

On the day of "The Accident," Danny and I were doing our things on Patrick's Corner. I remember I was shining the huge brown brogans that Mr. Clancy wore to his job as stationmaster for the N.Y.C. Danny was shouting something about General MacArthur and President Truman. I was dreaming, as usual, as I popped the shine rag in one of the many rhythms I had learned from Danny. Mr. Clancy leaned back against the barbershop wall and read whatever Danny was hollering about in his high tenor voice.

I didn't hear the bus in back of me until the driver locked the brakes and squealed to a stop. The abrupt halt actually shook the sidewalk as the heavy monster thudded against the curb and I could smell the rubber from the tires.

I turned, forgetting about Mr. Clancy, who had pulled his foot off the pad and was starting forward at a fast trot. In fact, most of the men and women who were waiting for crosstown transfers ran to the front of the stopped vehicle.

By the time I stood up from my shine boy crouch, the crowd was so thick I couldn't see anything at all except the backs of the people standing around the front of the bus. Danny, papers still in his hand, was jumping up and down trying to see over the crowd.

"Seán! Seán! What happened? D'ya know?"

I shouted that I didn't see anything. I resolved to wait until someone either got out of the way or told me what had happened.

I heard snatches of, "Is she hurt?" and "Did it hit her?" so I presumed (rightly) that someone had gotten their body in front of the bus and was, presumably, hit.

Danny could not stand the suspense of waiting. He set his papers down on the pile and shouted to me, "Seán-boy, watch me papers!"

There was no such thing as air conditioning on buses or in cars in those days. Bus windows were open and Danny grabbed a window frame and began to pull himself up. I was dumbfounded and scared.

"Cor! Danny, get OFF of that!"

Danny waved his free hand for me to keep quiet and continued to climb. He crooked his bare leg over the frame and lifted himself to the top of the bus. With an effort, because the metal roof was hot and slippery, he mounted the bus roof and began inching his way towards the front of the monster.

"Danny! Don't fall! Be careful!"

Danny was gingerly lifting his knees to keep them from scorching. He reached the very front of the bus and peered down to see what had happened. He obviously couldn't see, because I watched him spit on his hands to cool them and then lean very far over the brow of the bus.

Then he wasn't there. I was looking at my brother at one moment and, a moment later, he wasn't there!

A gasp arose from the crowd in front of the bus.

I screamed Danny's name and rushed and tore and pulled to get to the front of the crowd blocking my way.

Mr. Clancy saw me and lifted me bodily up and over the crowd.

Danny was lying on the pavement with his shoulder under the front bumper of the bus. His face was contorted and his eyes squeezed shut. Tears were streaming down his face but he wasn't making any sounds other than a soft "Ooooooooooooooooo," which escaped his lips as steam would escape the whistle-less teakettle in our house. His bare leg was folded under itself and stuck out at a very strange angle.

I rushed forward and held his shoulders.

"You hurt, Danny? You hurt?" I asked ridiculously.

"Ooooooooooooooooooooo!" The lady who was "hit" by the

bus was not injured. She actually had not been hit at all. She had started out in the street and stepped in front of the bus which, fortunately, had been able to stop before striking her. When the bus ground to a halt, she had been so frightened that she dropped the large bag of groceries she was carrying and passed out—dead cold—on the street.

Now it was Danny, and he was really hurt.

Pat and Tony arrived in the police car and transported Danny to the Saint Vincent. I rushed home to tell my older brothers—those who were home—what had happened. Mama was working at one of her "days" and Tommy went to get her. I was told to stay home and "put the potatoes on" while more competent persons took care of the serious business at the Saint Vincent.

It was almost eight o'clock when Mama, Tommy, and Danny got home. Danny's right ankle was wrapped in a white cast all the way to the knee. It looked very, very heavy and uncomfortable. Pat had gone back to the hospital and drove them home in the police car. I was full of questions, but Danny had been given some medicine and was not exactly up to conversation. Tommy and I got him to bed and he was quickly asleep.

"Mama?" I asked.

"What, Seán-boy?" Mama answered. Her voice was tired and she brushed her black hair back with her reddened hand.

"Should I sleep on the couch tonight?" was all I could think of asking.

"No. Just be careful not to bump the cast. Danny's going to be very sore for a while."

Life had other complications for Danny during his recuperation. He was a very demanding patient in a lot of ways. For the first two days in his cast, he spent most of the day lounging around and telling me to get him this or that. I did what he asked without complaining for a while.

Patrick's Corner was staffed by me alone for a couple of days. I would stack the papers next to my shine box and people would pick up their papers and drop their nickels next to my leg as I knelt on the sidewalk shining someone's shoes. We never really worried about someone cheating on us in those days!

Danny finally got tired of the forced isolation. The comic books had been read, reread, and read a third time. No one was home for long to play any games with him, and he hated Ma Perkins and Lorenzo Jones, the radio soaps of the day. Danny needed activity.

"Seán-boy, tomorrow I'm goin' to the corner with you. I can still hawk the news from my crutches and you can pass me a pile when I've sold my armload."

I didn't see any problem with that.

"You're doin' more than that, Daniel," Mama interjected. "You can go to school tomorrow, too!"

Danny tried to remonstrate, but knew it was no use. Billy, David, and Kevin were all at Holy Redeemer, where Danny was in the ninth grade. He'd have no problem getting himself and his books from room to room.

Kevin and I bathed Danny that night so that he wouldn't smell in school. My job was to hold his cast out of the water while Kevin soaped him up and poured a pitcher of water over his head to rinse the shampoo out of his hair. Kevin's dousing and my grousing didn't help his first bath since the accident. Later, Danny would learn how to shower by sticking his bum leg out of the tub while the water did the rest.

Danny's cast would stay on for six weeks. It got pretty dirty and was covered with autographs which time would make run together into great blue blobs. The doctor put a heel of some kind on his cast after a week or so and Danny discarded the crutches as quickly as he could upon learning that he could "gimp" along on the heel.

The one positive thing from all this pain and anguish was the fact that Danny was, for a goodly period of time, the center of attraction. People made way for him on stairwells at the apartment and at school. He delighted in telling and retelling the story of his plunge from the bus top, but never once mentioned the fact that it was just plain being nosy that got him up there in the first place.

After awhile, I got kind of tired of hearing the story over and over again.

I went with Danny and Mama to the doctor's office when the cast was removed. The doctor, a salty old medic with a little grey hair sprouting from an almost totally bald pate, took a huge pair of scissors and cut and hacked at the cast until he could spread it apart with his hands. The cast "popped" off of Danny's leg, leaving a dusty white limb, skinnier than I remembered, exposed to the elements.

Danny complained for a long time that the leg "itched" worse than it did when the cast was on.

Since we youngest boys usually wore short pants except to church and school, Danny's leg was clearly visible and showed several bruises and marks from the cast-cutting for a long time. The leg, compressed by the cast, was actually thinner than his "good" leg, but rapidly regained its shape and my brother was symmetrical again.

The strangest change was the fact that Danny became kind of quiet for a few days after the cast was removed. He was pleasant enough, but he wasn't the strong leader of all conversations, all situations, and all activities.

I think that he missed the cast and was having a hard time becoming center stage without his principal prop!

A couple of days after the cast was removed, Tommy commented on the bus incident at supper.

"Well, Dan-o," he said across the meatloaf Mama had made, "how does it feel to have both pins under ya again? Not back to mountin' busses, are ya?"

"Not for a while," Danny responded lethargically.

"Old Danny should wear a parachute to Patrick's Corner!" Kev added.

"Shut up, Kevin!" Danny spat out with such vehemence that it scared me.

"Daniel!" was all that Mama could say.

Danny finished his supper in silence and without looking up from the plate in front of him. When he had finished, he put his plate in the sink and went to the bedroom.

David and Kevin were the dish crew that night. Tommy

went out to visit his girlfriend and Billy walked Mama to the store for the things she needed for the next day's meal.

I went in the bedroom to see Danny.

"I got a new Action comic from Bloke today," I said as I entered the room. I held the book out as a kind of ice breaker.

Danny was lying back on the bed. His bare legs still looked different from each other, but at least the plaster dust which clung to his right leg for a couple of days had washed off. He was staring at the ceiling.

"Thanks, Seán-o," he said.

I sat on the edge of the bed flipping through the pages because Danny did not remove his arms from in back of his head to take the comic. I didn't say anything.

"I didn't mean to blow off . . . " Danny said after a moment of dead silence.

"I know it," I said.

"I kind of miss it, the cast . . ." he said softly.

"I think ya miss the attention," I ventured, stepping onto dangerous ground.

Pause.

"I guess you're pretty wise for a little shaver," he said.

"I get my own side of the bed back now . . . you've had it long enough."

"Let's go out and talk to Kev. I feel kind of bad about what I said to him."

We started out of the bedroom.

"Seán-o?"

"What, Danny?"

"You're a real good baby brother."

"Thanks, Danny."

Mrs. O'Quinn's Wake

WE PATRICKS CONSIDERED ourselves among the most charitable and loving persons on earth. There were few people we didn't get along with. There were few people we didn't like, and even with them, we tried to co-exist rather than indulge in conflict.

There were few exceptions. If the truth be known, however, there *were* exceptions. Sister Saint Mary was one, as far as I was concerned. Tommy had an active dislike for Kevin Hoolihan because Kevin literally "stole" Francie Egan— Tommy's first love—right from under his nose.

As far as I can remember, Gerard O'Quinn was the only person on God's green earth who was universally disliked by the Patrick legion.

The O'Quinns lived on the second floor of our apartment. We were on the third. The same inadequate kind of rooms we lived in were also shared by Gerard, his grandmother, and his parents. Gerard slept on a Murphy bed which folded down out of a closet in the family's living room.

Gerard was the same age as our Kevin. That would make him about fifteen at the time of his grandmother's demise. But I'm getting ahead of myself. (Danny has ALWAYS insisted that I could not tell a story, joke, or anything else in its proper order.)

We had lived in the small apartment for as long as any of us could remember. Tommy cut his teeth on the wooden railing on the "porch" which opened off our front room. I, being the youngest, would live there until my entry into the U.S. Navy at age eighteen.

The building had three floors with four apartments on each floor. Each apartment was identical except that the ones on the back side were turned around. Each apartment had a living room, kitchen, bath, and two small bedrooms. Each had a "porch," and each had an infestation of roaches.

In the winter, the entire building was heated by an ancient furnace in the basement which burned coke. Coke was a variation of coal which came in marble-sized chunks. It was usually the oldest Patrick's job to load the furnace stoker each morning and in the early evening every day. The next-to-oldest had the job of removing the "clinkers,"—large, hard objects formed from the burnt coke—and putting them in the metal barrels in the basement until trash day. Then we would all help carry the heavy barrels out to the curb for the rubbish men to collect.

Our family's rent—$45 per month—was five dollars lower than anyone else's because of this inconvenience.

The heat took a while to rise to the third floor, where we, the Murphys, the O'Malleys, and the Golnicks lived. Since we were the "heat people" and took care of the furnace, the landlord had the only thermostat in the building installed on our kitchen wall. We were the custodians of the heat for the entire building.

Since the heat took time to rise, we were the coldest. If we set the thermostat high enough to have adequate heat, the lower floors would be ten degrees higher than us. So, in deference to the first- and second-floor residents, the third-floor people usually wore sweaters in the house during the cold months.

The apartment dwellers were very conscious of the fact that we tried to please everyone and did the best we could. It was something that most of them were willing to live with. Sometimes they were a bit warm . . . at other times they would, like us, don sweaters for an hour or so until the ancient furnace did its thing and provided the heat we expected from it.

The O'Quinns moved into the apartment when I was seven or eight. That would make Gerard about ten because he, like Kevin, was two years older than I was.

During their first winter the O'Quinns made at least one trip daily to our apartment to complain about the heat. It was too hot and Mrs. O'Quinn expected her decorative candles in front of the shrine to the Virgin to melt . . . it was

91

so cold that Mrs. O'Quinn couldn't serve soup and keep it hot on the table while Mr. O'Quinn, Grandmother, and dear little Gerard ate their evening repast. . . .

Eventually, it was Gerard who was sent to our apartment with the heat/no heat complaints. He would rap authoritatively on our wooden door and then inform us that his mother (or father) (or grandmother) (check one wherever applicable) said that they were either freezing or burning up.

Gerard would have become the enemy even if he hadn't assumed the role assigned him by his family to protest the heat or lack of same. He was a repugnant-looking individual with an attitude to match. He was fat. He had brown hair which was generally falling in his eyes and which stuck out at various angles. We were sure that he didn't bathe and, as adolescence arrived, he developed a case of zits which we felt would be terminal.

Acne, to the Patrick boys, was a disease akin to leprosy. At the first sign of an intruder on a Patrick chin, the anti-pimple cream would be applied after several gallons of hot water and half a bottle of rubbing alcohol had been used to cleanse the area afflicted.

For a zit to become a "blackhead" was unthinkable. Once Kevin grew a crop of two or three minor zits on his chin overnight. He flatly refused to go to school and spent most of the day washing and staring in the bathroom mirror.

Gerard had zits upon zits. At least he did in our estimation. We were biased—that's true—but I really believe that I'm not wholly exaggerating.

Another problem with Gerard was that he didn't associate with anyone in the apartment. This was our world and we felt a kinship with the other residents. We had friends on the outside, but our fellow dwellers really came first.

Gerard hung around with the two Reilly boys, Buddy and Shane. They were (a) younger than Gerard, and (b) from Forest Street. Gerard never even tried to be friends with any Patrick, Dooley, Golnick, or other kid who lived in the apartment. He also never seemed to stay with kids his own age. They were always a couple of years younger.

All of these defects of character made Gerard someone who was considered weird and different and, certainly, not "one of us."

All Patricks were instructed, by Mom, to be polite to Mr. and Mrs. O'Quinn and, above all, to be respectful to Grandmother O'Quinn. Mom didn't insist that we be polite, respectful, or even sociable to Gerard. Frankly, I suspect that Mom harbored many of our own feelings for the troll of the apartment. She never said anything, though.

Grandmother O'Quinn was always "fightin' the _____ ." The name of the disease would be supplied as it applied at the moment. She was a chronically ill person as far as we knew. Mr. and Mrs. O'Quinn must have put up with a lot from her; retrospect brings a little understanding, at least.

After the O'Quinns had lived in the apartment for about five years, Grandmother really had a stroke. Pat and Tony took her to the hospital in the police car instead of calling for an ambulance. We imagined that secretly she was delighted to have had a genuine, honest-to-goodness stroke. It was, we figured, Grandmother O'Quinn's way of saying, "I TOLD you I was sick!" to her son and daughter-in-law.

She lay in the Saint Vincent for several weeks and then was brought back to the apartment. From the day she returned until her death a few months later, she never left the small rooms. We never saw her again. Mrs. O'Quinn told Mama one day that her mother-in-law was using a cane and was able to get around a little but could not speak clearly. That was the sum of our information.

On a Monday night in November Grandmother O'Quinn "went to her reward." She passed away without ceremony and without any warning. Mrs. O'Quinn found her cold and still on Tuesday morning. Herlihy, the undertaker, was called and took the old lady to his mortuary to prepare her for the wake.

In those days, wakes were held in the family home . . . or

93

apartment in our case. My Uncle Seán's wake had been held in our apartment less than a year before Grandmother O'Quinn's.

The body was delivered in the afternoon and the wake was to be held that night. Naturally, the funeral would be held the following morning because the art of undertaking had not reached the perfection of this day except at great and prohibitive expense.

Grandmother O'Quinn was laid out on her own bed. The undertaker provided several very large pans which were filled with whole cakes of ice and slid under the bed. The coffin, a frightening varnished box with a screw-on lid, was pushed in a corner of the room. Several vases of gladioles decorated the head section of the bed.

The wake wasn't anything like Uncle Seán's. His wake filled our apartment and smoke from railroaders' cigars wafted throughout the rooms. We remade the whiskey punch, which was served from the big soup pan, at least three times during Uncle Seán's send-off.

As we were residents of "the apartment," we were required to attend the wake of Grandmother O'Quinn. This was on a Tuesday night. None of us particularly cared to attend the wake, but considered that it was inevitable. I, especially, was offended because "Inner Sanctum" used to come on Tuesday nights. Danny and I literally lived for that radio program.

We went to the O'Quinns' apartment precisely at seven thirty, the official opening time for wakes in our neighborhood. Theoretically, they would last until ten o'clock. If the person was especially well liked and the wake was crowded, some of the people might still be in the family's home when funeral time came the following day!

We were required to dress for the event. We each had one pair of "dress pants" which, in the younger boys' cases, were usually the pair worn by the immediate predecessor the year before. Mine were third-hand tan trousers which were getting a little snug.

We each had a white shirt which was boiled after each

wearing and starched to a scratchy, cardboard texture. The collar always chafed my neck and I dreaded any occasion for which my white shirt would be required. Mom kept the white shirts in descending order in her own closet so that they wouldn't get soiled being stored with our daily clothing.

The last item of unique apparel was the necktie. Again, each of us had one. The older boys had ties which fit them and which they had to tie themselves. Danny and I had ties which came with an elastic band which fit around the neck and hooked just before the pre-tied knot. These ties were not very long and I felt we looked like fools whenever we wore them.

We arrived at the wake at the appointed time. Most of the regulars were already there—the Irish women who followed wakes like flies follow horses (as my brother Tommy used to say). There were a lot more people than I had expected, Grandmother O'Quinn being, firstly, an old lady who never got out much and, secondly, an O'Quinn. The second reason I identified with Gerard and felt that the unpopularity should run in the family.

There were folding chairs provided by the undertaker lined up against every bit of wall space. Not many of them were filled because the "regulars" would visit the deceased and then gravitate to the kitchen where the victuals and whiskey punch were being served.

We Patricks were not old enough to haunt the kitchen, although we would be allowed to step in to get a piece of cake before we left a couple of hours later. Instead, we were instructed to sit on the folding chairs and keep respectfully quiet.

I looked around the room. My brothers and I were the only young people there . . . except for Gerard. We sat in a line facing the bedroom where Grandmother O'Quinn reposed. I suppose it was all of the ice under Grandmother O'Quinn's bed that made the apartment seem rather cool. The room she was waked in was actually cold.

Mama came over to Tommy and whispered something to

him. He rose and left the apartment. When he returned a few minutes later Kevin leaned over David and Billy to ask where he had been.

"Mama told me to turn the heat up," he whispered back.

Mrs. O'Quinn had never exactly gotten the message that we considered her only child to be a wart on the fair skin of life. She led Gerard, dressed in a new pair of corduroys and an obviously brand-new shirt, over to the Patrick domain.

"Sit here with your little friends," he was instructed.

Gerard took the seat next to me, as I was at the end of the line and probably—being the youngest—posed the least threat to his manhood. I looked at Danny, who was trying not to giggle. My look told Danny that I sure hoped that zits weren't catching.

Kevin was the social butterfly of the Patrick clan. He leaned over Danny and me and attempted conversation with the Troll.

"So, Gerard, how goes it, the school?"

Gerard mumbled something which was garbled by having to pass through the field of zits. Danny was still trying to hide his case of infectious giggles.

We lapsed again into an uncomfortable silence.

Kevin suddenly got up and said, "I think I'll pay my respects to Grandmother O'Quinn."

I was a little surprised and a bit shocked. No one was in the room with Grandmother O'Quinn at that moment and I could not imagine anyone—least of all one of my brothers—wanting to be alone with a dead person.

Kev went slowly into the death chamber. He walked with forced dignity and went to the side of the bed where we couldn't see him. I imagined that he knelt by the bed and said a prayer or two for the safe passage of Grandmother O'Quinn to Eternal Glory.

It wasn't long before Kevin came back out. He paused by Gerard and said something about being sorry for his loss and then returned to his seat between David and Danny.

He sat for a moment and then leaned over to whisper something in Danny's ear. I could feel Danny starting to suppress his giggles again and saw his ear-to-ear grin, which he forced into a straight line as soon as he was able.

"What's up?" I hissed at my favorite brother.

Danny started to giggle again and it was a moment before he planted his mouth directly on my ear and whispered, "Under Gerard's chair. . . ."

I knew better than to look directly where I wanted to. I had to pretend to bend down to brush some imaginary spot on my polished second-hand shoes. When I bent over I looked. Under Gerard's chair was a good chunk of ice.

In back of Gerard's chair was a heat ventilator. This was breathing forth some very warm air after Tommy had gone to turn the thermostat up. The ice had only been under the chair for a few minutes and already was beginning to melt at an alarming rate.

I started coughing to cover the fit of giggles I was developing. Danny slapped me on my back . . . hard. He, too, was coughing and we didn't dare look at each other.

For the next half-hour we all—Gerard included—sat decorously in our line. From time to time I would sneak a quick peek at the ice, and saw that it was almost gone. In its place, a huge puddle was forming under Gerard's chair. It stood out vividly on the varnished floor and the edge of the carpet, which was under Gerard's feet, was showing a spreading dark patch.

Kevin got up again and said he was going to see if Mama wanted anything. He came back with a smug smile on his face. When he passed Gerard he muttered something about being sorry again. Kevin always had to overdo things.

Kev leaned over to Danny again and whispered something. Danny started to cough again.

I was about ready to poke Danny so I could find out what Kevin had said, but I was stopped when a rather tipsy Mr. O'Quinn strutted out of the kitchen. It was very evident that he had been sampling the pot of whiskey punch to anesthetize the pain of loss.

He staggered over to Gerard, looked at the floor, and shouted at the top of his voice, "Dammee, boy-o! Peed your

97

britches like a gosoon!"

Gerard literally jumped out of his chair.

"But, Daddy . . ."

WHAM! The meaty hand of Mr. O'Quinn found the posterior of his heir, and Gerard was jolted to the middle of the room. Mrs. O'Quinn came running in from the kitchen and tried to calm her husband, but he wasn't having any. "Get the gosoon a diaper!" Mr. O'Quinn shouted.

Gerard had wisely disappeared from the room.

Mama came in to see what all the hubbub was about. She quickly gathered her brood, expressed her sympathy again, and took us back to our now warm third-floor flat.

"But, Mama," Danny said on the way out the door, "I haven't had me cake yet."

"Never you mind the cake, Daniel. We've got some scones upstairs if you're hungry."

We had the scones and were all glad to turn in. It was late and we all needed to get to bed.

The lights were turned off, everyone said their prayers, and it was quiet.

"Kev . . ." Tommy said in a low voice.

"What, Tommy?"

"What did ya do to the Troll?"

Danny, my bed partner, was giggling so hard he almost bounced me against the wall. I stuck an elbow in his ribs, but that didn't stop his convulsive shaking.

"Got me a bit o' ice and put it right by the heat vent under his chair," Kevin said.

"You did, did ya?" Billy queried.

"I'm sure glad they like their flat warm," said David.

Danny continued to shake. I was getting a case of his giggles.

"Grandmother O'Quinn was kind enough to give me a chunk of her ice when I said it was for Beloved Gerard," Kevin said to the whole room. Everyone laughed and Mama hollered for us to be quiet.

"Then," continued Kevin between gritted teeth, "I went to the kitchen and told Mr. O'Quinn that it was a terrible thing how badly his Gerard was takin' his loss. I told him that the poor bugger lost control of his bladder he was so upset."

"Ya didn't, did ya?" Billy gasped.

"I did! What's more, I wiped my eyes in sympathy for poor Gerard!"

"Cor! You're a bugger yourself!" said Danny between convulsions of laughter.

Peace returned, broken only occasionally by one of us sputtering a giggle from time to time. Suddenly Danny jumped out of bed and went to the dresser against the wall.

"What's wrong, Dan-o?" Kevin asked.

"Changin' me underpants. I laughed so hard I think I peed 'em a bit meself," Danny said.

"Maybe Grandmother O'Quinn sent a little ice along!" David said.

It was a long time before we got to sleep. I was finally dozing off when Danny leaned against me.

"Seán-o?"

"What, Danny?"

"Check the mirror real careful tomorrow morning."

"Why, Danny?"

"To see if you caught any of Gerard's zits!"

The roomful of Patricks convulsed again. I rubbed my face all over Danny's back and neck before he pinned me back against the pillow. I could see his face clearly in the light shining through the window and knew he was laughing.

The Giver

IF MARCO WERE ALIVE today and still doing what he did best, he would be suspect of many improprieties. He would be looked upon as a "strange" person, at the very least.

Marco liked to play with kids.

We first met Marco shortly after the Second World War. He had served in the Army and had been wounded. His injury had left him with a lame, or "gimp," leg and he walked with a very pronounced limp.

Walking, for Marco, looked like a chore. He would step forward on his left foot in a relatively normal manner. Then, he would heave his right leg—stiff as a board—in a swinging manner, to get in front of the left one. This "swing" was kind of sideways and the right foot always landed completely on the heel.

Then, Marco would straighten up and start the whole thing all over again to make another step forward.

He always dressed in white—white pants and a white shirt. It was always a dress shirt too, and was immaculate. He either washed it every evening or had a closet full of Arrow shirts because this is the only kind of clothing I remember seeing him in.

Wherever Marco went a bevy of kids followed. He wasn't able to work and received some sort of check each month from the government in compensation for his wound. So, he had a lot of time on his hands and filled it with kids.

It didn't matter who you were or what stock you came from. Marco treated all kids the same. Italians, Irish, Jews . . . this was the majority of the neighborhood. We had a couple of Polish kids there, too. To Marco a kid was a kid and kids liked to play.

Summer was Marco's favorite season because the kids were home from school then. I imagine the hours during the school year were rather drab for this man who spent the greatest part of his waking hours being a friend to little people.

In the summer, Marco would invariably be at Patrick's Corner by eight thirty every morning. We would meet him and usually plan for some adventure which we would like to experience that day before we had to be home for our paper routes or shoeshine duties.

My older brothers missed Marco's years with us because they were out of the "playing" stage by the time he arrived among us. Danny and I, though, got the best of "the Marco years."

One of our favorite activities with Marco was to go to the large park which was several miles away. This meant that we needed two pennies of streetcar fare to get there and two cents more to get back. We usually budgeted a dime or so a week to provide for a couple of excursions and hoped that the weather would cooperate.

Park day was planned in advance. We needed to see how the group finances were, and some had to borrow from their allowances to have the carfare to participate. We also needed to get our parents' permission for these trips across town . . . and to be able to pack a lunch to take with us, as we would be gone the greater part of the day.

Mama must have trusted Marco because she never refused to allow Danny and I to go with him. We always had plenty of peanut butter, too.

Although all of our trips were memorable, one especially stands out in my mind. . . .

It was early summer and we were just getting used to the fact that we didn't have to be in the classroom listening to Sister So-and-So describing some incomprehensible subject, sweating in the heat of the sun which streamed through the dusty windows, and watching a lazy fly circling Mary Ellen Lafferty's desk in front of you. Freedom was indeed sweet, once you grasped the fact that it had arrived.

The day before the trip we had planned an extensive itinerary with Marco and the rest of "the gang." We had decided that we would enter the park at Lafayette Street and go all the way to the Lagoon, which was clear on the other side. The Lagoon was the area which we liked best. It was a clear, albeit small, lake in which Japanese Sunfish swam. There was a low stone wall surrounding the Lagoon and we could sit on this and dangle our bare feet in the water for hours watching clouds.

Near the Lagoon was the Devil's Kitchen. This area was really a large storm drain outlet that resembled a dark, forbidding tunnel to somewhere. Rumor had it that it went to the very bowels of the earth.

Danny and I were a little old for this kind of rumor but never contested it verbally, especially in front of the younger kids, because we remembered just how much fun it was to believe it ourselves.

Every trip to the Lagoon resulted in four or five boys— the girls never took part in this part of the escapade— marching daringly into the mouth of the Devil's Kitchen and going as far as they dared before turning and running back to the entrance. The first dozen feet or so of the tunnel wall were covered with initials indicating just how far each brave soul got before marking his name and running out.

Trip morning dawned bright and warm. It would be a scorcher before noon that day. Danny and I rose before the rest, except for Tommy, who had to work early, and dressed in our shorts and t-shirts. We spread peanut butter thickly on Mama's homemade bread and wrapped the sandwiches in waxed paper. Danny found two apples in the icebox and put them and the sandwiches in our cloth "knapsack," which was really only a sort of pouch with a strap which could be thrown over one's shoulder. I got our "war surplus" canteen, which we had bought from John the Hardware (we called him that just as if it were his real name. His first name was John, and he ran the hardware store. It made sense to us) for thirty cents, and filled it with cold water. This I hooked on the waistband of my shorts and thought that I looked the part of a real explorer.

Most of the group had already assembled by the time we got to Patrick's Corner. Marco always took a list and, with the stubby pencil he always seemed to have, wrote the names of all the children he was taking with him. He also collected the carfare for the trip both ways. The money for the trip to the park would be put in the right-hand pocket of his white trousers. The money for the return trip would be wrapped in a handkerchief, tied in a knot, and placed in the left-hand pocket.

The streetcar arrived and we piled on. That day there were about fifteen kids, mostly boys, but a couple of girls as well. We passed the conductor and his fare box and Marco reached in his pocket and dropped the whole batch of pennies in the machine. This was always the procedure when we went with Marco. No conductor ever questioned it. Marco never varied it.

I loved to ride the streetcar, with its clattering rails and sweet-smelling wicker seats. We pulled all of the windows open and sat in twos and generally in the back.

I always liked the very back seat, which stretched across the whole car. I would usually kneel on the wicker seat and watch the guy rope of the trolley, which rose up to meet the electric power lines above the street. When we would reach Hardin Street, the conductor had to get out of the streetcar and pull the rope to guide the trolley to the proper power line which would take us in the direction we were going.

When we arrived at the park that day we got out of the streetcar and waited for Marco, who was always last. He swung his leg off the car and came to our group. This was "Order Time."

"O.K.," he would say, list in hand and sweat already forming on his low-browed forehead, "we stay together . . . no exceptions. I'm in front with Danny and you, Ritchie, and Seán take the rear."

We were the oldest. Marco and Danny would lead the pack and Ritchie Lieberman and I, both twelve, would guard the rear, making sure that no one fell behind. That done, we entered the park and proceeded at a leisurely pace towards the Lagoon.

Our park was really beautiful. Families used to take their children there on Sundays. Several areas had stone grills where charcoal fires could be built and meals prepared.

103

The wooden picnic tables had a lot of initials carved on them but, to my knowledge, were never broken or vandalized.

Pathways were all through the park and the large oak, maple, and elm trees provided cool shade as we walked them. The park was full of squirrels and other small animals which scurried out of the way as Marco's army trudged upon their domain. Every so often, a stone fountain with a metal spigot would be found, spouting a continuous flow of clear, awful-tasting water. Our area was apparently rich in sulphur because the water had a pungent taste of the chemical. We used to say that if one held his nose he couldn't taste it. Danny and I always carried our "war surplus" canteen, though.

It was about ten o'clock when we reached the Lagoon. Our pace was slow because we enjoyed looking as we walked and because Marco's leg wouldn't carry him as fast as our young and healthy legs could carry us. We kept pace with Marco, our leader.

Every so often, too, someone would holler "Halt!" to see some animal or some burrow and the group would stop. The entire crew would look over whatever we stopped for and, when all had seen what there was to see, we would gather back on the path and march on.

"Mercy Stops" were made in much the same fashion except the one who needed the stop would scamper off behind a tree and the rest would wait until he reappeared.

On this particular day, a Wednesday, I think, the Lagoon area was deserted except for us. Most of the boys immediately removed their shoes and socks—if they wore them—and waded in the shallow water or tried to "tickle" fish by lying on the low stone wall and dangling their hand in the water, hoping a fish would happen by their fingers.

Marco, Danny, and I sat on the slight slope which rose to a grove of trees which crowned the hill overlooking the Lagoon. Ritchie Lieberman and a couple of younger boys asked if they could go to the Devil's Kitchen to look at the initials.

We must have been there for an hour or so and had eaten our peanut-butter sandwiches already, when Marco became a little concerned about the Devil's Kitchen crew. They had been gone for quite a while and it was time to check on them. Marco wasn't really worried because Ritchie was twelve and had always been very dependable.

Danny and I volunteered to go look for them because Marco's leg would hamper the climb he would have to make and the subsequent descent to the storm drain itself was a very rocky way, indeed.

We trotted up the hill and reached the edge of the minor cliff which descended to the Kitchen. As we looked down, we could see Terry Hogan and Walter O'Brien sitting on one of the large boulders strewn near the entrance to the tunnel.

"Yo! Terry and Walter," Danny called. "Where's Ritchie?"

"He's in the Kitchen!" Walter called back. We hurried down the rocky terrain.

"What d'ya mean that he's in the Kitchen?" Danny demanded.

"He went in there and told us to wait here for him," Terry explained. Terry and Walter were about nine years old and were good at taking orders.

"How long's he been in there?" I asked the guys.

"Ever since we got here. We were thinkin' of coming to tell Marco."

"He's gonna find where the Kitchen lets out," Terry said. "He don't believe that it goes direct to Hell, he don't."

Danny looked at me. Then he went to the mouth of the tunnel and called Ritchie's name. It sounded like Danny's clear voice trailed down the tunnel and died. We waited for Ritchie's response. Nothing happened.

"I'm goin' in the tunnel and go to my initials and call," Danny said. "To where the dark gets bad."

I remembered the day that Danny and I went deep in the tunnel and scratched our initials with stones on the wall. Danny went a couple of feet beyond me to prove that older means braver. I remember I was very afraid being that far

105

in the tunnel. After scratching our initials, we turned and ran like the very devil was chasing us out.

"I'll come with you," I said to my brother.

"No, Seán-o. You wait with Terry and Walter. I'll not go farther than my initials, so you should be able to see me all the while."

He went into the gaping jaws of the Kitchen and hurried at a trot to where we could barely see his white legs and T-shirt. I heard Danny's tenor shout Ritchie's name, but it sounded like he was a long way off. He called again and there was another pause. Then Danny came running out. His legs were splashed with dirty spots from running through the slim river of water which was in the center of the wide tunnel.

"We better tell Marco," he called as he reached the entrance. I spun on my toes and climbed the rocky cliff and went to tell our leader.

When Marco heard what Ritchie had done he called Margaret Mary Kenney to him and put her in charge of the younger kids. He told the group to obey her and told her to keep everyone in one place until he got back. Then, without hesitation, he climbed the long slope leading towards the Devil's Kitchen.

Navigating the "cliff" which led to the creekbed that the Kitchen opened into was a major feat for Marco with his game leg. He did it, though. A couple of times his leg went out from under him and he would slide on the dirt and sharp stones for several feet before he regained his balance. I tried to hold him a couple of times but my small stature was not enough. I do believe that I lessened the damage, though.

"Danny!" Marco called as we reached the entrance to the tunnel. "You take these two back and help Margaret Mary take care of the kids. Seán, you come with me. We're going to find Ritchie."

I blanched. Marco was telling me that I was going to go into the very jaws of certain doom! He didn't even wait for an answer because he started off in his gimping pace directly down the center of the tunnel at the fastest trot I had ever seen him travel. Danny looked at me. I had no choice. I shrugged. I started off after Marco and looked over my shoulder at Danny leading Terry and Walter back up the "cliff."

I caught up with Marco and had to move swiftly to keep up with him. As we walked, the water in the tunnel got slightly deeper and splashed on Marco's white trousers and on my bare legs.

"When it gets too dark to see well, Seán," Marco said, "put your hand on the side of the tunnel and hold on to my belt with your other hand."

It was plenty dark, all right. I planted my hand on the side of the tunnel wall and grasped Marco's belt with my left hand. Every so often Marco would call Ritchie's name. After an eternity of sloshing on and calling his name we were rewarded by a faint "Here!" from a great distance away.

Marco stopped dead in his tracks and called again. Once more the faint "Here!" sounded.

"Let's move very slowly," Marco told me, "and hang on to me. It sounds like Ritchie got himself into one of the side tunnels. . . ."

I hadn't even known that there were any "side tunnels" in this great bastion of hell. They were, in fact, feeders from various other places. As we moved slowly I suddenly felt open space instead of the wall that my hand had been sliding along.

"Here, Marco!"

Marco faced the invisible opening and called Ritchie's name again. This time it came back fairly strong. We were going in the right direction.

"Remember that we turned right off of the main tunnel," Marco cautioned me. We headed slowly down the pitch-black tunnel, stopping every several feet to call Ritchie to get our bearings.

After an eternity, Ritchie's voice was directly in front of us. When we reached him, he hugged Marco and told us that he was lost and thought that he was a "goner" for sure.

Marco had me make a complete turn to face in the direction from which we had come. He led, Ritchie hooked his hand in Marco's belt, and I hooked mine in the waistband of Ritchie's shorts. Single file we started the long trek out.

We made the proper turn when the side tunnel met the main storm drain and before long could see the pinpoint of light which indicated the mouth of the Devil's Kitchen. We let go of each other and walked three abreast the rest of the way out.

When we reached the end, I could see that Ritchie was a mess. He had obviously fallen in the water several times. His legs were scratched and his elbows were bleeding. He had been crying, too. Great streaks of dirt ran down his cheeks. Even his hair was a mess!

Marco stood guard while I helped Ritchie clean up at the fountain in the grove at the top of the hill. We took his shirt and soaked it and used it to sponge his face and body with. Then he held his head under the lower spigot and I ran the sulphur-smelling water through his hair.

When Ritchie was relatively presentable we went back to the group. Ritchie answered a million questions, Marco delivered a lecture on staying with the group and I was looked on as a sort of hero for daring the very bowels of hell to consume me on my mission of mercy.

The conductor looked a little strangely at Ritchie when we boarded the streetcar for the trip home. No one wanted to sit with him because of the collection of smells he had acquired. Danny and I sat with him on the bench seat, though. The Devil's Kitchen, we felt, smelled worse than Ritchie, anyway.

Marco continued to care for the neighborhood kids. Long after I had gone to the navy Marco would be shepherding a new generation of children to the park, or to the local playground . . . giving the only possession he really had: himself.

Marco was occasionally thanked. From time to time a child would bring him a small gift, especially at Christmas when he assembled the kids for caroling. But he never really wanted anything except the one gift which was universal among us . . . and our parents. He was given the trust that the children were in good hands. The trust that they would all return a little better off than before they left. The trust that they would be guided, chided, and encouraged by the little Italian man with the white shirt, white trousers, and gimpy leg.

This gift he freely accepted.

That night, after the descent into the Devil's Kitchen, I was tired. I showered even though it was the middle of the week and put my play clothes into the hamper for Mama to wash. When I went to bed I felt the friendly cool of the sheets and the faint breeze from the open window. Danny and I didn't even want a sheet over us that night.

"Seán-o?"

"Mmmmmmmmmmm?"

"What was it like in the Kitchen?"

"I don't even know, Danny. I was so scared I had to think to keep from wettin' my britches!"

"But it was dark, wasn't it?"

"Oh, yeah. Dark as a very tomb. I had to feel along the wall, it was so dark. When we found Ritchie I couldn't even see him."

"You're a brave one, baby brother!"

We were silent for a moment. Suddenly I sat bolt upright on the bed and leaned over my brother's face.

"Danny!" I hissed, and shook his shoulder with my hand.

"What's wrong, Seán-boy?"

"I forgot to do it, Dan-o!"

"Do what?"

"To put my initials where we stopped!"

"COR!" Danny almost shouted as he sat up and hugged me to him.

"Quiet in there!" Mama's voice came through the door as Kevin opened it to see what was wrong.

Danny and I both laughed and lay down to sleep.

The Egg

I HAVE NEVER BEEN a fan of eggs. I have gone so far as to call them "unborn chickens" and launch into a diatribe about allowing them to "grow up" when they could be eaten as drumsticks, thighs, breasts . . . Provençale, Kiev. . . .

Eggs, to me as a child, were an unnecessary evil which we could have for a meal instead of food. And have them we did. At least a couple of times a week our diet consisted of heaping platters of scrambled eggs which were augmented by fried or boiled potatoes. On occasion we would even be offered this dubious luxury for breakfast.

My family—myself, my mama, and my five older brothers—lived on the edge between abject and utter poverty which occurred shortly after the Great Depression. Mama did her best to supply the necessities for her brood of fatherless Irishmen, and did a credible job of it. As we grew older and could earn a few dollars, we would each contribute to the family grocery cart, and a greater variety was had by the Patricks of Maxwell Street.

Still, certain things were inevitable. We had meat only once or twice a week. We had chicken (real, meaty, and with bones inside chicken) every Sunday because one of us always worked for the live poultry store on the corner of our street. We had potatoes for virtually every meal except breakfast. And . . . we had scrambled eggs at least twice during the week for supper.

Skippy O'Byrne's dad was an eggman and usually gave us several dozen cracked eggs without charging for them. The rest we would buy for seven to ten cents a dozen. They were fresh and Mama scrambled them in a heavy cast-iron skillet which we called a "spider." Grease which was carefully saved from our infrequent meals featuring bacon was the ingredient added to assist the scrambling process.

Eggs again, I remember thinking on Tuesday and Friday

nights. Life had few mysteries even for the baby of the Patrick brothers.

I had a brief rebellion against "hen fruit" one time. It was quite a satisfying experience, too. Nothing spectacular, mind you. Just a rebellion that only a ten-year-old could conjure up in a relatively unfettered mind.

My rebellion took place on a Wednesday morning and was really over before I had gotten to school. But it was out and out warfare for the "gosoon" of the family.

Mr. O'Byrne had given Mama a surplus of eggs the night before. We had our usual scrambled egg supper and quite a few of the whitish orbs remained. We, like most of the families in our decaying apartment building, had a real "ice box." Not many people whom we knew could afford the newer electric refrigerators which kept food fresh and cold without the addition of a chunk of clear, cold ice. No, ours was, like our friends', a large, wooden "ice box." The top had a hinged lid which would be swung open to accommodate a large chunk of ice which was delivered every few days by Jerry on his horse-drawn wagon emblazoned on the side with the legend: "City Ice and Fuel."

Jerry would "park" in front of the apartments and throw the heavy canvas tarp back to reveal a wealth of ice in huge blocks. He would chip a heavy chunk off and, with the meanest-looking tongs man has yet devised, hoist it onto his leather-protected shoulder and carry it to its destination.

I loved ice day because we would "hang" by the wagon and catch the chips which flew from Jerry's ice pick. On really hot days Jerry would be moved by some strange Angel of Mercy which liked small boys, look around as if to be assured that no one was looking and hand each of us a good-sized chunk of the precious gemstone ice to suck on and rub over our faces and chests.

Back to my egg rebellion.

We had limited storage for things in the ice box and Mama thought that her boys would enjoy the treat of a boiled egg for our breakfast on Wednesday. When we had dressed and found our way out of our six-boy room or the crowded bathroom to the kitchen table, we were greeted by what was to Danny and me an unfamiliar sight: whiskey glasses at our places.

Breakfast for the Patrick boys was usually a bowl of cold cereal in the warm weather or a bowl of warm cereal in the cold. My favorite was Wheaties, but Rice Krispies ran a close second in the cold cereal department. Oatmeal was the only warm cereal I believe had been invented when we were kids.

We both stared in awe at the six whiskey glasses on the table . . . those and a spoon at each place. Mama was standing at the stove with the potato-pot at full boil.

"Cor! Mama, what's the shot glasses for?" Danny the Bold wanted to know.

"Mama's gonna send us to school smellin' like we been in the Old Bushmill's!" Billy, who was fourteen, said, referring to the bottle of Irish whiskey Mama kept under the kitchen sink in anticipation of Uncle Michael's visits.

"Never you mind your mouths!" Mama cut them off. "The glasses are for puttin' your breakfast egg in."

Sure enough, Mama lifted the eggs, one by one, out of the pot and put one in each shot glass. She laid a second egg in front of each of us on the table. We were, she informed the youngest of her offspring, to crack the top off of the egg, salt and pepper the mushy mess inside, and eat that with the spoon which was provided.

The older boys, who had obviously had this kind of treatment before, went to it with either feigned or real gusto. Tommy especially looked like a pro. He took his spoon and, with one expert whack at the egg, decapitated the little fellow and began the salt ritual. Billy, David, and Kevin were pretty good, too.

Danny and I watched. Danny tried the one-swing method and succeeded in knocking the egg out of his whiskey glass and onto the table, where it lay intact and none the worse for wear.

Tommy helped Danny and Billy offered to help me.

"I ain't eatin' an egg for breakfast!" I protested.

"Breakfast is cereal and I don't want no egg."

Enough had been said. I was looked at by my brothers and then ignored. If the gosoon wanted to go hungry that was his problem. Mama saw it differently and pronounced sentence.

"You'll eat the eggs and like 'em," she said.

"I'll not!" I countered.

"Seán-o, eat the bloody things," Kevin said. Mama told Kev to watch his mouth.

I sat mutely. No more words would pass my lips. Tommy, Billy, David, Kevin, and Danny could sacrifice principle for conformity, but not this bucko.

Mama struck the death blow.

"Seán . . . think of the poor starvin' children in Europe . . ."

This was the line which was used to force us to eat the unedible. The phrase which could open the most tightly pursed lips and allow liver to pass through. The truism which caused even Danny to endure cottage cheese or David to drink buttermilk.

Our minds would conjure up masses of urchins huddled together with earthen bowls held pleadingly in front of them. They had no hair and their eyes were set so deeply in their sockets that they were almost invisible. They were also almost naked, but we didn't tell anyone that for fear of being accused of enjoying what we conjured up.

That was the last straw. I stood up and took my egg from the whiskey glass and marched wordlessly into the bedroom. This in itself was an act of bravery because the thing was HOT and I almost dropped it. I did drop it on the bed as soon as I was safely out of sight.

My school books were on the bed waiting for me. I dug in my jacket pocket and fished out my Wearever fountain pen. Across the egg I boldly printed:

To: The Poor Starving Children

Europe

113

This done, I marched to the kitchen cupboard with immense dignity and opened the drawer where things like string, rubber bands, writing paper, recipes, and postage stamps were kept. All eyes were on me as I found a purplish three-cent stamp with George Washington's picture on it.

"I'll pay for the stamp when I shine shoes tonight!" I announced and marched back to the bedroom. There, I licked the stamp and pasted it on the still-warm egg, which I put in my jacket pocket.

David, Kev, Danny, and I were all still at St. Columbkille school, and walked there together.

"What did ye do with the egg, Seán-o?" David wanted to know.

I didn't answer.

"C'mon, Seán-o!" Danny insisted. We were just at the corner where we crossed to go to school.

The mailbox stood sentinel-like. I walked over to it and pulled the egg out of my pocket. I held the stamped orb up so that David, Kevin, and Danny could read the address . . . and then I dropped it in the mailbox.

"I didn't put me address on it so's they can't send it back!"

I crossed the street with the trio of puzzled Patricks following in their baby brother's wake.

"Cor!" said Danny.

"Hey, Seán-o! Wait up!" Kevin called and hurried to my side.

"What, Kev?"

"D'ye think that a stamp'll stick to liver?"

I thought it would, but that it would be hard to address with my Wearever fountain pen.

I still don't like eggs.

The Graduate

SISTER SAINT PATRICK SPARED no effort in getting us ready for graduation from Saint Columbkille School. Actually, she spared no effort in getting us ready for anything that we were to do. She was a tried and true perfectionist who spent a lot of energy making certain that we would always show our best side no matter what the occasion.

I guess to her, and certainly to Mama, graduation from Saint Columbkille marked more than just an ending of attendance at one school and the beginning of another. Mama considered sending us all to Catholic school to be one of the main obligations of parenthood—and this in the days when the ten-dollars-a-year tuition for each of us was not easily come by.

The week before the actual graduation was a sort of hodgepodge week of planning, of relaxing, and of doing things we never dreamed were possible in the hallowed halls of Saint C's.

The eighth-graders had their final exams a week before the rest of the school, so we were really finished with our academic careers while the rest of the underlings plodded on with tests and things like that. We, the elite about-to-graduates, had to be there, but were involved with such ethereal endeavors as going over to the Church to practice for the ceremony, listening to Eileen O'Donnell give her speech over and over until we all knew it by heart, and sandpapering the edges of the textbooks we had used so they would look neat and almost new for the next class who would sit in our lofty places.

I think that Sister Saint Patrick felt the twinges of nostalgia as much as we did. Our class, just like the multitude of classes which preceded us, was the "best class" she had ever taught, the "most promising," and the epitome of "what Saint Columbkillians should be," she told us in her endless monologue during the day.

We practiced until we were perfect, marching slowly—heel, toe, heel, toe—down the long center aisle, imagining where our families would be sitting and trying to keep our pride from showing too much. Then, humming "Pomp and Circumstance," we would be dismissed early, a prerogative and privilege of eighth graders, and walk slowly home being nostalgic and very adult since we knew that "everyone" was watching us.

Graduation day was the only day of the year when the rigid schedule of Saint Columbkille was changed to suit an occasion. The ceremony was held during the ten o'clock Mass and the eleven o'clock Mass was cancelled to accommodate the length of the festive event.

On Sunday morning, I got up early and went in the bathroom before anyone else was up so that the earthly body of the graduate would be spanking clean. I dressed in my new white shirt and long blue pants, tied my dark blue tie, and slicked my short hair back with unnecessary Brylcreem before the bathroom was invaded by my brothers, who were hurrying to get ready for the Mass.

We didn't wear caps and gowns like they did in high school. The only mark of distinction—besides the blue pants and tie—was the pair of long ribbons in Saint Columbkille green and gold which we pinned to our shoulder. The girls wore white dresses and had the ribbons, too.

I remember feeling nervous, like the first time I served Mass, as we waited outside the church for the procession to begin.

Mama and my brothers, except for Tommy, who was helping protect Korea with the navy, were about midway in the packed church. Danny winked at me and I looked quickly away so that I wouldn't start giggling . . . a problem I still have during stressful moments.

The Graduation Mass was always a solemn High Mass with Monsignor Hanratty as celebrant, Father O'Phelan in his usual deacon position, and Father O'Toole as subdeacon. High school boys served the Mass but, since I was graduating, none of my brothers was pressed into service for the job. The altar looked somewhat strange, I thought, without a single Patrick assisting at the Mass.

At the end of Mass, Finneran and one of the servers pulled a long table into the center of the sanctuary with the boxes holding our rolled diplomas. Then Sister Saint Patrick, looking like she was losing her own children to the lions of the Coliseum, introduced Eileen O'Donnell, who gave her speech about going out into the world full of confidence and fearless zeal.

There were a lot of graduates, so things were moved along swiftly. Monsignor Hanratty gave a five-minute homily about how proud he was and then started giving out the diplomas.

As each name was called, the graduate bearing that name stood and walked—with immense adult dignity—to the sanctuary where he or she received the diploma, shook hands with the Monsignor and with Sister Saint Patrick, and then walked proudly back to his or her place. The Monsignor always said, "Congratulations, (Name), and may God bless ye. . . ." as he shook the graduate's hand.

I sat fidgeting through the first half of the alphabet waiting for my name to be called and praying I wouldn't trip or something on my trek to the sanctuary for my diploma and handshake. Bloke—whose last name began with "C"— wiggled his diploma at me when he came back and Mike Polanski, sitting next to me, hissed that he bet Bloke's was signed in disappearing ink.

Finally, after the incredible number of "O"s—O'Brien, O'Casey, O'Connell, O'Donnell, O'Farrell, O'Leary, and the rest—I heard my name called and almost tripped getting out of the pew.

Monsignor Hanratty held my diploma in his hand and smiled at me as I reached for it and held my right hand out for my handshake and "God bless ye" from the impressive pastor.

"Ah!" he said, departing from the routine speech, "Here we reach the end of the line. . . ."

He stood there holding my diploma as I waited, holding my breath and praying he would get on with it.

"Saint Columbkille is blessed with many large families,"

he said at my expense, "and it is always a moment of reflection when we reach the end of the line. Seán here is the last of the Patricks in our school, so we'll have to try to get on without one now, won't we?

"Oh, they'll still be with us . . . young men in high school, in college, in the nation's service. But, even so, it's the end of the line—the last of your children, Mrs. Patrick, to go through our school."

I could hear Mama clear her throat in the silent church. She always did that when she was nervous.

"It's a proud moment for ye, Kate," the Monsignor said in a kindly tone, "and I know ye miss Tom and wish he was with ye as the gosoon of your family gets on with his life and goes on to high school.

"Aye, Kate . . . I miss auld Tom, too. But I know he's lookin' down from his place in Heaven with tears of pride in his eyes when he sees the fine job ye've done with his sons."

Sister Saint Patrick stood by smiling and I could see old Father Guilhooley sitting in his chair in the door of the sacristy nodding his head as Monsignor Hanratty spoke.

He finally handed me my diploma and traced the sign of the cross over my head before reaching for my hand to shake.

"God bless ye, Seán-o," he murmured as he shook my hand.

I turned and marched, crimson-faced, back to my place and tried to scrunch down in the pew because I knew everyone was looking at me.

After graduation, we marched back to our classroom for the last time to get our holy card from Sister Saint Patrick and then we went back outside to meet our families to walk home.

Mama immediately grabbed my diploma to make sure it didn't get soiled. She would put it in her drawer with five other Saint Columbkille diplomas, and already two from Holy Redeemer High.

"Let me see your holy picture, Seán," Mama said as we walked home.

I handed her the card bearing the familiar image of Saint Patrick and she turned it over to look on the back.

"What did she write?" I asked as I heard Mama chuckle

while she read Sister's message.

She handed me the card.

"To Mr. Seán Liam Patrick," I read the fine Palmer Method penmanship. "I have looked after you long enough and it's now time for a rest. May the good Saint Patrick now step in and guide your steps for the rest of your life! In J.M.J., Sister M. Saint Patrick."

I smiled and remembered Sister Saint Edna, Sister Saint Mary . . . all of the nuns who had chided, goaded, and prodded us through eight years of more than just education. I knew that even though she had signed the card, it was written with all of those formidable women of God in mind. Saint Patrick would certainly have his work cut out for him!

I still have the card.

We had a little family party the evening of my graduation day and I was kind of glad when everything was over and I could take my necktie off.

"You know," I said to Danny as we muddled around the room getting ready for bed that night, "I'm gonna miss the old Saint Columbkille. . . ."

"I missed it, too, for a while," he said, "but it was a sort of fond missin'. You'll like high school, though, once you get used to it."

"What's it like, Dan-o?" I asked my next older brother.

"Oh, it's a grand, big place, the Holy Moley . . ." he told me, using the affectionate nickname for Holy Redeemer High. "Maybe a bit scary at first, but you'll get used to it. Hang your good pants on the hanger or Mama'll kill you."

I hung my good pants on the wooden hanger.

"Don't be afraid of it just because it's big," Danny went on as we got ready for bed. "It's not so big that it can't use another Patrick."

"Even one who's the 'end of the line?'" I asked with a smile.

"Especially one who's the end of the line!"

Spreading the Good Word

ONCE A YEAR—IN THE FALL, I think—we used to have this big competition between all of the Catholic grade schools in our city to see who could sell more subscriptions to the weekly Catholic newspaper. It was a big event and the schools would get a percentage of the subscription money to use for athletics and things like that. There were prizes in each class for the student who sold the most, too.

The newspaper was not really the greatest thing since the advent of movable type. It usually consisted of a lot of stuff about what Catholics were doing all over the universe; about what was going on in the parishes of the diocese; about the CYO football or basketball leagues; and about what the Knights of Columbus were doing to raise money to help this or that cause.

Still, it did give locals the chance to see their names in print if they had done something in their parishes. It also carried the weekly "Legion of Decency" ratings for the movies being shown in the theaters so that we would know if we were excommunicated or not if we saw one.

For those among you who aren't aware of the Legion of Decency ratings, the organization listed movies as "G," which was O.K. for the whole family to watch; "A," which meant that the adults could see it and still be relatively moral; "OP," or "Objectionable in Part" (I guess that meant that it had some sexy scenes in it); "O," which was completely objectionable; and "C" for "Condemned." The only "C" movie I remember by title was *From Here to Eternity,* and that's currently being shown on TV during prime time every couple of months or so. Times have changed.

Anyway, we had to sell these subscriptions to the newspaper every year. The thing cost two dollars for a subscription, which was no small amount back in those days when the hourly wage started at twenty-five cents.

We always had a big pep rally in the gym before the drive

120

was "kicked off" in the school. Sister Saint Kermit, the principal, held the paper up for us to see and hollered about how essential to salvation it was for us to read the thing. She displayed the different prizes we could win and told us, in effect, to go out there and "win one for the Gipper!" She always ended the rally by telling the story of the legendary Eileen O'Grady, who sold 100 subscriptions in a single week. It was no small feat and a goal to be reckoned with!

We were given a half-dozen subscription blanks, a copy of the newspaper, and the admonition to storm the city and to beat the sales of any school which would dare to compete with Saint Columbkille.

Mama got her subscription from us in descending order. The first year she bought from Tommy, then Billy, David, Kevin, Danny and, finally, from me. Kevin's suggestion that she buy two subscriptions in case one got lost in the mail fell on deaf ears.

We Patricks were always way up in the sales department because we had a "Plan of Action" which was always a carefully guarded secret. Tommy, our oldest, had discovered it and we kept it under wraps as we progressed throughout the years. While our classmates traipsed from door to door, duplicating the efforts of their friends and annoying the already subscribed customers, we concentrated our assault on the one bastion of buying humanity in our derelict neighborhood . . . the Shamrock Pub.

The Shamrock, as it was called, was a small drinking man's bar next door to Chris's Barber Shop on busy Hardin Street. It was smack-dab in the middle of the intersection which we called "Patrick's Corner" because of our shoeshine and newspaper hawking businesses there. Because of its location, it was indelibly stamped as Patrick Territory and was thus safe from interlopers.

Tommy originally had reasoned that if an Irish Catholic was a fairly easy sell for the local Catholic newspaper, an Irish Catholic with a couple of snorts of Jameson's Whiskey was an even easier sell. History would prove him accurate in this estimation, to the benefit of us all.

Most of the men in the pub knew the Patrick boys. We had been on the corner for a lot of years and they were used to seeing us. Whenever Danny had difficulty getting rid of his regular evening papers, he would trot into the bar and holler "PAPER!" and usually get rid of his excess in a matter of minutes. Kevin, the best athlete of the family, was well known, too. His success in the CYO boxing tournament was discussed annually by the patrons and it was rumored that a goodly amount of money traded hands when the men would bet on his victory and in what round it would occur. Tommy and Billy were also very good football and basketball players in high school and these men were avid fans of both sports. So, Patricks were considered "good kids" and were generally welcomed and patted on the back by the bleary-eyed patrons of the Shamrock.

We would hit the bar together, three of us at a time. Inside, we divided up the bar and the couple of booths and went from patron to patron displaying our sample copy of the paper and explaining how informed a Catholic would be if he subscribed. Usually the clincher of "it would be disloyal to the pope if you don't subscribe" was not necessary.

The men would dig into their pockets or would scoop together the loose bills and change on the bar and dictate their names, addresses, and parish affiliation to the Patrick who stood before them. After the first couple of sales it became easier, as the men farther down the bar knew what was coming and had their two dollars ready before we got to them.

One year Mr. Hoolihan subscribed three times on separate days because he had forgotten that he had just purchased a subscription the day before. Kev got the first one and failed to tell Danny and me. Danny got him the second day and I got him on the third. Since he was an office worker on the New York Central we reasoned that he made a lot of money, and didn't feel too badly taking some from him. Nonetheless, three times was a lot and we tried not to repeat that for fear of alienating the clientel.

Another time, a watery-eyed patron named O'Malley

insisted on buying a second subscription from me because he had a brother named Seán back in Ireland and felt that it would be a tribute to this gentleman who was fighting with the IRA to buy one from a good freckle-faced kid who bore his fine Gaelic name.

Back home, we would divvy up the subscriptions and put the money into our envelopes to turn in at the end of the week. Mama never knew where we had been and always complimented us on our dedication and effort in "spreading God's Word" to the resident Irish of the neighborhood.

We never had to regress to the door-to-door stuff to out-sell most of our classmates. The good sisters used to remark how faithful we were in that the addresses on our turn-ins represented such a wide cross-section of the city. We sat quietly and accepted the accolades as our due while classmates like Bloke Callahan and Dale O'Leary glared their intimate knowledge of our fertile territory, but never said a word to our detriment.

The sisters were right. We were good. No doubt about it.

Ralph's Miracle

THE DAY WAS VERY, VERY WARM back in 1960. My shipmates and I had found a little sidewalk cafe just outside the gates which marked the beginning of the "Domaine"—that non-commercial, eerily other-worldly area which is Lourdes. We could see the Basilica in the distance and watched the thousands of pilgrims shopping for candles, souvenirs, and the like in the multitude of shops which dotted the main street which led to the Grotto.

"Sure wish we'd see a miracle while we're here," one of my companions muttered.

I would have liked to have seen one, too, I thought. One of those dramatic affairs when a cripple would rise up off his stretcher and walk . . . a blind person gasp as the rays of God's sunlight streamed into his formerly unseeing eyes. . . .

"Those things don't really happen anymore!" another sailor said. "They ended with the Bible."

"No, they didn't," I said softly. "They happen all the time."

No one heard me, but that was O.K.

When our visit was over and the bus was reeling through the Pyrenees, taking us back to our ship, I reflected that I had already been blessed by witnessing a miracle many years before. And, I thought, I had probably witnessed a thousand more while we stood before the niche in the hillside where the Mother of God had appeared more than a century before.

Ralph D'Agostino was a friend, a classmate, and a real neat kid in our neighborhood. He was Kevin's age, which made him two years older than me. Like Kevin, Ralph was a popular boy and a skilled athlete. He played on the football and basketball teams at Saint Columbkille's and, later, at Holy Redeemer High School. It was a common sight to see Kev and Ralph walking home in the twilight with their gym

124

bags swinging loosely from their hands and their hair still damp from the showers after practice for whatever sport was in season at that time. Neighbors would wave to them and call "Hi!" as they passed because it was well known that the success of Holy Redeemer was due, in a large part, to their skill and daring on the athletic field.

I was about to become a freshman at Holy Redeemer and Kev and Ralph were entering their junior year when Ralph's illness struck. At first he just felt ill, but he quickly became progressively weaker and unable to leave his house. The local doctor, who visited him almost daily, shook his head and finally took Ralph to the hospital, where he had tests done for almost a week. We were glad when we saw the taxi bring him home, but more than a little disturbed to see his father and brother literally lift him out and carry him into the apartment.

"Got some kind of blood sickness . . . like a cancer or something," a dejected Kevin told us at supper. "They've been givin' him medicine but it don't seem to help him much."

Mama went over to talk to Mrs. D'Agostino and came back with the unsettling news that Ralph indeed was a very sick young man and that Mrs. D'Agostino had asked for help in storming Heaven in search of a miracle.

Our nightly family Rosary added, from that day on, a steady petition for Ralph's well-being. Mama began one of her Novenas to the Sacred Heart of Jesus, and I remember often catching myself unconsciously praying "Dear God, please make Ralph well!" several times during the day.

After school started up again Brother Paul, the principal, often included a mention of prayers for Ralph during his daily announcements over the P.A. in the classrooms. This was a serious business, indeed!

Kevin was a regular visitor at Ralph's apartment and Danny and I accompanied him a couple of times. I remember being totally unnerved after my first visit when I saw our athletic friend lying in his bed. The flesh had literally melted from him and the bones of his face gave him a

125

chiseled look. His bright eyes were sunk deep in the sockets, which were outlined by dark, shadowed circles on his pale skin.

"Only a miracle will save him . . ." I overheard Mama saying one day to Mrs. O'Malley. I resolved to work towards that end from that moment on.

Our school library had several books about miracles and, especially, one about Lourdes. Danny and I read the book about the wonderful things that had occurred and put our faith in the Lady of the Grotto, praying as often as we remembered for her intercession and a miraculous cure.

Kev spent more and more time over at the D'Agostino apartment and we would look up when he came in for some encouraging sign. Usually, though, he would just shake his head and kneel with the rest of us for the Rosary.

Ralph died just before the traditional football game which pitted Holy Redeemer against Saint Ignatius from the other side of town.

By Wednesday the school was decorated with posters and banners proclaiming the havoc our Lions would cause to the "enemy" on Friday evening. The atmosphere was almost festive as we slapped the varsity players on the shoulders when we passed them in the halls, telling them how great they were and what we expected of them on Friday.

I had put my jacket in my locker and wandered aimlessly into homeroom. Bloke Callahan was completing a "Go Get 'Em Lions!" sign on one of the blackboards as the bell rang and Brother Tesclin whooshed in, waving us to our seats. Usually we began our homeroom period with a short "Hail, Mary" and the Pledge of Allegiance, but Brother Tesclin told us to be seated as the P.A. crackled to life.

We were all looking at the little box on the wall next to the crucifix as Brother Paul's voice projected hollowly over our heads.

"It is my sad duty to inform you this morning that one of our own—Ralph D'Agostino of Homeroom 3-D—passed into the loving arms of God during the night. . . ."

He had begun leading the school in a communal prayer

for our friend, when I felt a gigantic hiccough erupt from my throat and I suddenly—and loudly—burst into tears, burying my face in my arms, which were folded on the desk. I was embarrassed for crying in front of my classmates, but I couldn't stop. I could hear the murmured prayers and felt Bloke's arm around my shoulder. When I finally looked up I saw a lot of others wiping their eyes with handkerchieves or on their sleeves, so I didn't feel so bad.

I went through the rest of the morning in a sort of daze, but so did a lot of others. We had never really experienced the death of one so close and so young before. At lunchtime I got my bag with my sandwich from my locker and headed to the cafeteria. Kevin was coming out of the bathroom as I passed and our eyes met. I could see that he had been crying, too.

"Kev. . . ." I wanted to say something but didn't know what.

"It's O.K., Seán-o. It's O.K." He hurried on to his class and I went to eat my peanut-butter sandwich.

Brother Tesclin caught me as I was getting my books to take home after the last class. Our freshman football team didn't have practice on Wednesdays, so I was going to go straight home. Danny, Kevin, and David, all on the varsity team, would be late.

"Come on with me, Seán-o . . . you, too, Bloke!" Brother Tesclin motioned for us to follow him and a couple of other freshmen classmates towards the gym.

The varsity football team was assembled on one of the bleachers in the gym and Coach Bostick was pacing in front of them. They were suited up for practice and most of them were bobbling their helmets in their hands. Brother Tesclin told us to sit down. I looked over at the team and saw Mr. and Mrs. D'Agostino sitting on the first bench. Mario, Ralph's older brother who had been a great football player at Holy Redeemer, was there, too.

Coach Bostick said some consoling words to the family and told the team how much he felt our collective loss. Then he said that Mr. D'Agostino had something to say. The burly man who paved the city streets looked uncomfortable in his suit when he stood up. He had a piece of paper in his hand.

"Our son, Ralphie, is gone home to God," he said softly, "and we all will miss him very much."

I was hoping he wouldn't cry, because I felt like I would start all over again if he did.

"So many of you were his good, good friends. He was very lucky to have had so many.

"He went suddenly. One minute he was with us and the next one he was gone. He knew, though, that he was dying last night. After Kevin left Ralphie told me to write down what he wanted to say to you and here it is. . . ."

He waved the little sheet of notebook paper in the air.

"Kevin, you were his friend in a special way. Would you read this for the team?"

Kev clomped down from the third row of seats and took the paper from Mr. D'Agostino. He cleared his throat.

"Dear guys," Kev read softly, "I sure wish I could play with you against Ignatius. You guys will do great, but watch out for Foley, their halfback. He can run!

"I know that you've all been praying for a miracle—that I would get well. I hear my mother talk about it with my dad. I've prayed for one, too, for a long time—ever since I got sick."

Kevin's hand was shaking a little as he stood in front of his team reading the note. He cleared his throat again and went on.

"But it's O.K. I got my miracle. I'm not scared and I'm not sad anymore. God knows what He's doing and that's the most important part. I talk to Mary and I really think that sometimes I hear her talking back, telling me that she's waiting for me and that she'll hold my hand when I meet Jesus."

Perhaps it was coincidence. The high windows of the gym blazed with the sudden fall sunlight and it streamed down on the floor, beaming directly on Kevin. His white practice uniform seemed to glow as he read the end of the note and he had to shade the paper with his hand to see the writing.

"I feel good, really good," he read, "and I can't wait to watch Friday's game! I'll be watching from a very special seat, guys, with a lot of new friends . . . but I WILL be watching! I love you guys a lot. Your buddy, Ralph."

Kevin handed the paper back to Mr. D'Agostino. The gym was totally silent and I heard the soft voice of Brother Tesclin muttering:

"Oh, glorious! Glorious!"

The team went out to practice and we went up to shake hands with the D'Agostinos.

Ralph was buried at Saint Columbkille on Friday morning. Almost all of Holy Redeemer was present for the funeral. Monsignor Hanratty ignored the fact that Ralph was not really a child and wore the white vestments for the "Mass of the Angels" instead of the traditional black for a Requiem.

We had a pep rally that afternoon and things felt a little more like they were beginning to return to normal. At the end of the rally Coach Bostick said that the team was dedicating the game to Ralph.

At Lourdes, a half-dozen years later, I thought about the miracle I had witnessed. It was, in effect, as great a miracle as any I could have imagined. The drama of instant healing was not present, but the immense courage, the blazing faith, and the confident placing of a young boy's unquestioning trust in the unseen hands of God and His Mother was an overpowering affirmation that a miracle had, indeed, been granted.

I thought about the thousands of pilgrims I had seen that day at the Grotto. Some of them might experience physical healing, I reflected, others might not. Whatever the outcome, I knew that the miracle of faith was alive and well. I had seen the peace and the loving trust radiating from the stretcher-prone pilgrims just as I had seen it beaming from the D'Agostino family in the Holy Redeemer gym.

The game was exciting that Friday night. It was a close game and we won by only two points when Kevin and C. J. Amato dropped the Ignatius quarterback in his own end zone for a touchback.

I will always remember my view from the stands where I sat near the D'Agostino family. As I watched the game unfold in front of me I was watching the bench, as well. The players would jump up when the coach told them to go in, and they would trudge back as they returned from the field, plopping down on the wooden plank with a thud. It was obvious, though, that they carefully kept one seat clear. In a single, open space in the sea of gold jerseys, a lone helmet with the number 32 rested on the seat.

Once, during the game, I watched Kev trotting off the field pulling his helmet off. Billy Rafferty, the manager, tossed him a towel to wipe the perspiration from his face. Kevin stood wiping his face dry and tossed the towel back. He started for his place on the bench, when he stopped and glanced at Ralph's conspicuously vacant spot. Kev grinned and gave a quick, two-finger salute to the helmet, and I instantly knew that Ralph's miracle was more far-reaching, and the healing more complete, than we could have ever hoped for.

The age of miracles over? You can bet your boots—or football shoes—it's not!

The "Holy Moley"

JUST AS ST. COLUMBKILLE SCHOOL had Patricks in classrooms for about a thousand or so years, the same pattern evolved at Holy Redeemer High School. However, since Holy Redeemer had only ninth through twelfth grade, we only populated the school for eight consecutive years.

Holy Redeemer was a forbidding edifice on Seventy-Third Street. It took up the greater part of the block on frontage alone and the school seemed to extend for miles in the rear. It was, as Danny told me when he was preparing me for my venture into the world of high school, a "grand, grand school!"

As with most northern industrial cities of the time, our city had a vast number of Catholics and Irish. There were, at the elementary level, as many parochial as public schools. We had fewer high schools, but they were always the power-houses in all athletics and were entered only through academic competition. They also cost money to attend. Fifty dollars a year, to be exact. That was a substantial sum when one figures the number of children of school age in the Irish Catholic population!

The Christian Brothers ran Holy Redeemer, which was the nearest all-boy school in our area. Our Lady of Perpetual Help Academy was the girls' school in that same neighborhood. Virtually all of the St. Columbkille alumni were expected to attend these two bastions of learning, depending on their sex.

To get back to the Christian Brothers, they were a no-nonsense lot who wore long, black cassocks and little bib-like white collars. The long, dress-like cassock didn't fool anybody. We knew that under the clerical garb existed a world-class prizefighter who would stand for no foolishness in his classroom.

These brothers took a certain verbal beating from every class of freshmen that entered. Almost all of the fledgling ninth graders had spent eight years (or more, in the case of Bloke) being educated by nuns in one of the many diocesan elementary schools. It took most of us several months to overcome the habit of answering, "Yes (or no), Sister," in the classroom or in private conversation with these academic men of God.

Holy Redeemer was commonly referred to as "Holy Moley" by its students. By those of us raised with pidgin Irish speech patterns common in the family, it was more properly referred to as *The* Holy Moley. None of us knew how that particular appellation came to be applied, but it had and that's what we called our school.

I was luckier than a lot of kids. Most freshmen wandered around the halls for the first couple of days of school trying to discover where they were supposed to be. Many of them fell victim to the sellers of "elevator passes" ("to help you get to the upper classrooms on time with an armload of books") in a school which had no elevator. I had three older brothers in school when I entered. David was a senior, Kevin a junior, and Danny a sophomore. They shepherded me around the first couple of days and made sure I was where I ought to be and there on time. They also made known to their more enterprising friends that Seán-o knew that there was no elevator and not to bother him with that trash.

Thanks to my older brothers, too, I was never stigmatized by having purchased a school "duffel bag" with the HR emblem emblazoned on the side. They did look attractive and most freshmen bought one for two dollars to carry their books in. Danny told me, however, that it was common to refer to a new student—a freshman—as "a stupid look and a duffel bag." Enough said.

Fortunately, our reputation was somewhat better at The Holy Moley than it had been at St. Columbkille. For one thing, we had a lot of different teachers. We changed classes every period and no one brother was hit by a full day's concentration of a Patrick staring at him. The nuns taught the whole grade and had to look at the same faces all day, every day. That can make one grim, I guess. (One brother, Brother Joseph, did have four of us in a row one year. He taught religion classes and had David for third period, Danny for fourth, I was in his fifth period, and Kev wound up his day during sixth period. He never let on that it bothered him, though.)

My whole high school career was somewhat bland. I played on the football team, as I played on St. Columbkille's. I was there and didn't do anything spectacularly good or bad. In fact, I played Offensive Right End again. I did swim on the school team, though. I was quite a good swimmer. Since our school didn't have a pool, we had to practice at the local YMCA, which was a block away from school. I turned out to be a fair swimmer and diver.

Kevin, however, was active in just about anything he could get into. He was a three-letterman in football, basketball, and baseball; he edited the school paper and was on the Dance Committee; he tried out for the school play but didn't get picked during the auditions; he was in the Math Club (to which I never aspired), and was president of the Student Council during his senior year. He was also the one who let the chicken loose during the Honors Day Assembly.

That feat would still be legend if Holy Redeemer were still in existence. I suppose that there were louder events, like the pep rallies before city championship games, but Kev's chicken has got to hold some record for an academic occasion.

I was there, too. I was a freshman and attended all school functions, since they were generally held during the school day. Sometimes they would have split assemblies, with juniors and seniors attending one performance and the freshmen and sophomores attending another, but most of the assemblies and rallies were held for the whole school.

We had a large, old, and very impressive auditorium. We didn't use the gym, as most of the other schools in our city had to, because we had a real auditorium. It had theater-type seats on a sloping floor and a large balcony which overhung approximately one-third of the room. The stage had professional lighting (I operated the light board during the school play my senior year), and massively heavy curtains which parted with an audible *hissssss* as they were electronically opened. It was a top-notch theater.

The theater, though, was the scene of most of the major disruptive events at The Holy Moley. Catcalls, false farting, and all of those things could go on almost undetected because the student body of two thousand was crammed into the theater and only a few of the Christian Brothers ever bothered to patrol the aisles. Robert Hogan used to bring a supply of paper drinking cups into the theater in his gym bag and pop them with his foot, making a loud, gunshot type of noise during certain assemblies he didn't like.

We did, on the other hand, have a couple of musical entertainments which were very good and no one made any disturbances during those. Our own concert band had their concerts there too, and they were nice to listen to. I used to watch the drum section because they had a lot of flair. Teddy Finucan played a xylophone-like instrument called a marimba and used to perform solos every time the concert band had a concert.

"Educational" assemblies were either very good or very bad. One time some men from the local General Electric plant came and talked about electricity. They had a whole bunch of experiments and things to demonstrate with. They even made artificial light just like lightning bugs make by pouring a couple of chemicals into a large bottle. Then they had everyone in the first couple of rows hold hands and they turned a large wheel which caused all those holding hands to get a mild shock because they were connected together. I was glad I was not in the first two rows.

The other kind—the awful kind—of assemblies were those where someone would stand and talk for sixty-three hours about some author or other. I even took part in the burping and fake farting during those assemblies.

Anyway, we had this annual event called the Honors Day Assembly. This was when those who had done especially

134

well in the various subjects would get medals and certificates. The whole school had to turn out to see them get these things. I guess it was to make us all try harder to be like them.

Actually, the assembly was a really nice thing. Some Patrick usually got a medal or a certificate for something. During this one, in fact, David was given a one-year scholarship to the Jesuit university in our town for being outstanding in Latin.

The assembly began like all the others. We sang the alma mater and the principal, Brother Paul, started in his usual fashion: "Your Excellency, (the bishop was always there on the stage for Honors Day), Reverend Clergy, Honored Guests, Fellow Faculty, Men of Holy Redeemer . . . and Freshmen."

This was supposed to be funny and all the sophomores, forgetting that they had sat where we were sitting last year, hooted and laughed a bit to show their appreciation to Brother Paul that they were no longer ". . . and Freshmen." When I was a freshman I thoroughly hated Brother Paul's standard introduction and all of the sophomores who laughed. I was sure that Danny never laughed at this.

He spoke for several minutes about how the honors were justly and diligently earned and then he felicitated (that's the word he always used instead of "congratulate") the award winners and turned the assembly over to the heads of the various academic disciplines.

Seniors got their awards first and that took quite a while. I was getting very antsy waiting for the whole thing to get over with and needed to go to the bathroom anyway. I had my pencil out and was rolling it around in my fingers trying to survive the interminable naming of Mr. So-and-So for this or that.

When I think back I vaguely remember hearing a very hushed commotion from the balcony where the juniors sat. It was only momentary, though, and I didn't make any great note of it. Brother Patrick kind of looked up for a second from his patrol station in the aisle next to my row, but it was a casual look and he promptly returned his gaze to the more important matter of who had won some medal.

One of the seniors who was to get an award for math was Cornelius Regan. You'd think his nickname would be "Corny," but it wasn't. Regan, the star halfback of the city's championship football team and heavyweight boxing champion in that year's CYO boxing tournament, was nicknamed "Chicken." Everyone called him that and he always answered to it. It was certainly not derogatory as far as he . . . or we . . . were concerned.

"Chicken" Regan was one of those people who are very gifted both academically and athletically. He was also a very nice guy and never tried to be a big shot or anything. Even I, a lowly ". . . and Freshman," could wave at him and call, "Hi, Chicken!" in the hallway. He knew a bunch of my brothers and would always throw a quick wave in my direction and maybe even a "How's it goin', Seán-o?"

Brother James, the boss of the math division of the school, was calling out several awards and scholarships for the seniors who had done well in that discipline. When he got to Chicken's name he called out, "Cornelius Regan!"

Chicken started to walk to the stage (seniors and others who were to receive awards were seated in the back of the downstairs section of the auditorium so they could walk up to the stage and be seen by all), and had gotten about half-way to the stage when a real commotion broke out in the balcony. A whole bunch of Juniors started chanting, "Chicken! Chicken! Chicken!" and making clucking sounds. This did not apparently upset Chicken, because he broke into a very wide grin and started to look up at the balcony.

Then everything went to pieces. Someone threw a white object a little bigger than a football in the air from the bal-cony. I thought it was a wad of newspaper at first.

It was a live chicken.

The chicken, in mortal panic, began flapping its wings for all it was worth as it plummeted down to the first level. It landed on several heads and flitted from person to person in its psychotic and frantic attempts to get out of its predicament.

Just as panicked were the students among whom the chicken had landed. Strong and brave Sophomores clawed each other trying to get out of the way of the frenzied fowl, who was flapping and screeching for all to make way. Several dropped on the floor and tried to cover their heads. Others bravely pushed, stepped on, and shoved fellow students in attempts to escape a possibly vicious pullet.

Eventually someone caught the chicken and took it out of the auditorium. Several Christian Brothers made beelines to the balcony to apprehend the culprit who had spirited this bird into the hallowed halls of Holy Moley. The bishop, on the stage, was actually trying to stifle a laugh and had his hand up over his mouth so that we wouldn't know that he thought the thing was funny. Brother Paul was mortified.

The rest of the assembly, after the dignity of the occasion was somewhat restored, went off quickly and smoothly. We ended as we had begun, singing the alma mater. I would learn several years later that the bishop confessed that his class at Holy Redeemer (he was an alumnus) had turned a cat loose in a chemistry class, but had not had the courage to loose a chicken during an Honors Day Assembly.

"Chicken" Regan took the attention as an honor and was very flattered that he had been selected for this singular distinction.

We laughed about the event at home that night. Billy, who had graduated last year, said that he wished that his class could have thought of something as original as that. Mama said, after a slight frown indicating that she was outwardly supporting strong discipline in schools, especially Catholic schools, that someone ought to write a letter to Tommy, who was with the navy in Korea, because it would give him something to have a nice laugh over.

Billy asked if anyone knew who had smuggled the chicken into the auditorium. None of us had any idea. We figured it must have been carried in under someone's shirt or something.

We were still joking about it when we got ready for bed that night. David had gone over to a friend's house and would be home later. Billy was sitting with Mama listening to a radio show. Kevin, Danny, and I were going to bed and were jostling around the bedroom as we hung our clothes on the hooks on the wall or threw them in the large basket which served as a hamper.

"Cor! Dan-o, did you see that chicken zingin' down from the balcony?"

"I thought they could fly better than that," Dan-o said and poked my bare stomach with his balled fist.

"Can chickens fly?" I asked Kevin, who I figured would know since he was the one who was working at the live poultry store at the moment.

Kevin was standing in his underpants with his back to us looking down at his stomach. He apparently hadn't heard my question.

"What, Seán-o?" he asked as he turned towards us.

His whole midsection had red scratches on it. They didn't look bad but there were a lot of them. They looked like a bunch of chicken scratches. They looked almost like Kev had had a chicken under his shirt. . . .

"What, Seán-o?" Kevin asked again. He smiled his sideways smile and broke into a Patrick grin.

"Nothin', I guess, Kev," I said. I sidled over to my grinning brother and gave him a goodnight kiss on his cheek. Danny did the same thing and hopped into our bed.

Kevin walked over to the light switch, turned towards us, and flexed his muscles. He also flexed his stomach muscles, which made the reddish marks stand out like stripes.

"'Night, brothers!" He grinned and flicked off the light.

There were a couple of giggles from the peanut gallery.

"'Night, Kev!"

"'Night, Kevin."

". . . cluck!"

"Who said that?"

138

Duffy

DUFFY'S DEATH STRUCK all of us with a blow which will last for the rest of our lives. He was "one of us."

Duffy wasn't his real name. He was born and baptized Dorian Fitzhugh, the only child of Megan and Red Hugh Fitzhugh who were friends of my family and, I believe, who came from the same county in Ireland as Mama. Duff's mother, Megan, died shortly after his birth. Mama and a few of the neighbors in our derelict apartment building attempted to help Red Hugh with the care of his child, but Red Hugh sank into a depression at the loss of his Megan and soon felt it best to send young Dorian to an aunt's home in Pennsylvania where he could be raised properly. Red Hugh, himself, became a lonely, almost never-to-be-seen hermit appearing only for his work as a fitter at the railroad roundhouse, or seated by himself in the rear of the Shamrock Pub, where he spent his non-working/non-sleeping hours.

Duffy was about twelve when his aunt's own health began to fail and he was returned to live with his father. Like Red Hugh, Duff was a loner from the very start.

Kevin was Duffy's age and was in the same class at St. Columbkille School. Kev, the social butterfly of the Patrick clan, attempted several times to make friends with this hapless youngster, but usually met with little enthusiasm. Kevin's daily, "So, Duff, how goes it?" was usually greeted by either silence or a mumbled response.

"Cor, Mama! The bugger's a lonely sort. He eats his lunch by himself and sits on the fence at recess. After school he goes to his flat and isn't seen 'til school the next day!"

Kev could not—would not—tolerate a cold response from any being with warm blood flowing through his veins. Duffy's rebuffs only tantalized Kevin, who brought the problem to the family table one evening.

"Why don't you invite him over for supper with us?" Mama asked.

"D'you think he'd come?" David queried.

"I can't but ask," Kevin said. "Mama, what are we havin' tomorrow?"

Mama told him we were having cod and boiled potatoes. We had this frequently on Wednesdays and it was one of our favorites.

The next evening Kevin appeared with a reluctant Duffy in tow. He later confided that it had taken considerable diplomacy to get Duff to agree to come, but that he had finally relented.

Supper was especially fun that night. Tommy kept up a steady string of jokes, usually aimed at Billy, who played the straight man with charm. Duff sat on the long bench-seat between Kevin and Danny. I sat balanced uncomfortably on the end of the bench. I liked Duffy from the start.

Duffy and Kevin became close friends. This would continue throughout their high-school years at Holy Redeemer. Like Kev, Duff was a natural athlete and the two became a sort of legend for their prowess on the basketball court at "The Holy Moley." They double dated and Duff became a fixture in the Patrick household. Many nights I would climb out of bed in our six-boy room to make my way to the bathroom only to step on Duffy, who was wrapped in a blanket on our bedroom floor.

"Cor! Seán-o, watch where you're steppin'!"

"Sorry, Duff. I didn't know you were here."

After graduation, Kevin entered the Fire Academy to follow in Billy's footsteps as a fireman. Duffy entered the United States Marines. He wrote several times during his training and, at its completion, was sent to Korea. Tommy was there, too, with the navy. We wondered if they would run into each other.

One Friday Kevin came home from the Academy for the weekend and found a letter from Duffy waiting for him. We looked forward to Duff's letters as much as we did those of Tommy. Kev tore it open and read it aloud.

"I really like the people here. It's a very pretty country in its own way . . ." he read. "I am making a lot of new friends and feel that I am doing a good job as a Marine."

Duffy never failed to ask after "the young bucks," as he called Danny and me.

That Saturday morning Danny and I had to get up early to go to our jobs at the market. We jostled around the bedroom trying valiantly not to disturb David, who had been up late studying for one of his examinations in college.

When we went into the kitchen we saw Kevin seated at the table with a mug of cold tea in his hand. Mama stood next to him and had her hand on his shoulder. Duffy's letter from the day before was lying by his elbow. Mama gestured for us to be quiet.

"Dorian's dead," she said flatly. "Kevin met Red Hugh at the Shamrock last night and he told him."

"Didn't bat an eye, he didn't," Kevin said tonelessly. "Killed in action. Cor! He said he heard yesterday from the government. The bloke didn't bat an eye!" Kevin's voice was rising. "God, Mama! Duff hasn't even anyone to cry for him!"

A shudder rippled suddenly across Kevin's broad shoulders and the first sob that came rose from the very depths of his soul.

"Arrrrrgggghhhhhh! Ye bugger! Ye damn bugger, Duff!" Danny and I rushed to Kevin and grasped his arms.

"Dammee! Duff! Duff! I loved ye an . . ." Kevin shouted into his arm, where his head was buried. Words ceased and he gave himself over to the agony of mourning. I realized that tears were streaming down my own face and that Danny's was contorted with rage and sorrow.

When Kev had calmed, Danny and I let go of his arms and he sat up slowly. The strength was returning to his voice.

"I loved him, Mama. He was like another brother and I'll miss him so much. . . ."

Mama didn't answer. She had moved over by the window and stood with her back to us. She held a corner of her apron up to her eyes and her shoulders were gently heaving as she wept for a "son" who would never come home.

141

Kevin had been wrong. Duffy indeed had someone to cry for him.

Duffy was buried the next week. The Marines had sent an honor guard, who fired a salute over his metal coffin and who handed a folded flag to Red Hugh, who stood uncomprehendingly by the gravesite throughout Monsignor Hanratty's ritual.

After the service, when the honor guard had gone, we prepared to leave the cemetery. As we reached Billy's car Danny noticed that Kevin was not with us. We looked back and saw him, a solitary figure, standing at the grave looking at the grey metal box Duffy now lay in.

No honor guard had ever stood so tall.

Danny and I went to get Kevin. We approached quietly, not wishing to interrupt this moment he so needed. As we drew near we could hear Kevin's soft voice.

"So, Duffy. How goes it, ye bugger?"

I'm sure Kevin heard an answer.

The Caretaker

MR. COLEMAN AHEARN WAS a "frightening auld man" to us—
my brothers and I—when we were youngsters. He lived all
alone in one of the only real houses sandwiched between
the tenement apartments of which our neighborhood was
made.

Mama told us that Mr. Ahearn had lived in that house
long before my family had moved into the neighborhood.
She said that she seemed to remember that Mr. Ahearn had
had a sister who had lived there with him, but that she had
died many years ago.

The house was enough to give a boy a case of the "chills"
or "chicken skin" if he stayed long enough to really look at
it. First, no sun even touched it. The house was wedged
tightly between two six-story brick apartment buildings,
which blocked any effort of the luminary to rest on it. Secondly, it had been built at about the turn of the century,
which would have made it about fifty years old when I had
the chance to meet its owner and to learn about things
which I would remember the rest of my life.

"He's a Dallahan with a head!" Danny pontificated one
day at the supper table. A "Dallahan" is a sort of headless
ghost who does no one any good—not a more acceptable
spirit or fairy such as a leprechaun, who makes shoes, or a
Cluricaun, who gets drunk in people's cellars and just
makes noise. A Dallahan was something not quite pleasant
and certainly to be feared and avoided.

"Don't be dumb," said Kevin who, at a year older than
Danny, obviously knew more. "He's just an old man who
doesn't like people and wants to keep to himself."

Tommy, Billy, and David kept their thoughts to themselves. I guess they felt that we "young blokes" could busy
ourselves with this nonsense.

"He's an auld man who needs prayin' for," Mama finally
said in an effort to terminate the discussion. "Mr. Ahearn

has been here longer than any Patrick and has a right to his privacy."

We thought that she had finished. She paused for a full moment and then said as she turned back to the stove to scramble more eggs, "Still, 'tis strange that he's not even seen in the Church anymore. I remember he used to be like clockwork at the 5:45 on Sunday mornings. . . ."

Irish Kennedy was full of local legends, and he had told us in strictest confidence that he had it on good authority that Mr. Ahearn had murdered his young wife nearly fifty years previously and had buried her in the basement of the house. He would never, ever move from there for fear of the body being discovered and his heinous life of crime exposed.

Coleman Ahearn was among the most diminutive of men, which gave some credence to the "legends" of his being in cahoots with the leprechauns and other "faerie people" so dear to an Irishman's heart. Barely five feet tall—if that —he was also stooped, presumably with age. On his very infrequent trips to the local grocer he could be seen walking slowly, bent over an ancient blackthorn walking stick—a shillelagh. A small tweed cap rested on snow-white hair, which he obviously cut himself. His jacket was, like the cap, tweed and hung loosely on his gaunt frame. His trousers were usually brown and he wore heavy-looking brogans on his feet.

On those days of Mr. Ahearn's shopping, which seemingly occurred only twice a month or less, neighborhood children, myself included, were certain to avoid the side of the street Mr. Ahearn was walking on. He carried an empty cloth shopping bag in his free hand. This was usually full on his return trip, presumably with groceries for his sustenance for the remainder of the month.

"What does he buy?" I asked Billy one time. Billy worked at the small grocery where Mr. Ahearn and most of the neighborhood women shopped.

"Cor, Seán-o!" I don't know what he buys. I'm busy with the customers and stockin' the shelves when he comes in.

I've no time to be watchin' a bloke get his groceries, and you shouldn't be worried about someone else's business, either!"

It's not easy being the youngest.

Even our friends who lived in the apartments on either side of the ancient two-story frame house were left to wonder what Mr. Ahearn was about, because they told us that he kept all of the blinds tightly drawn over his windows.

Our meeting with Mr. Coleman Ahearn happened suddenly, unexpectedly, and in a most unusual manner.

Kevin, Danny, and I were playing stickball in our street with Bloke Callahan, Irish and Fuzzy Kennedy, Rich Saperstein, and Seamus O'Donnell. This was the way we usually passed the time on warm summer days until it was time for Kevin to start his paper route and for Danny and I to go to Patrick's Corner to hawk the newspapers and shine shoes as the crosstown trolleys and busses evacuated their passengers at the end of the working day.

Rich had just hit a "liner" which evaded Seamus's lunging dive. Seamus took off down the street after our only ball and Rich trotted the bases with ease. This gave us all the opportunity to breathe for a moment. I leaned against my pole and noticed Mr. Ahearn plodding his way, leaning on his blackthorn stick. The shopping bag swayed heavily from his free hand. I was glad that I was on the opposite side of the street, although most of my "fear" of him had vanished when I turned thirteen a month before.

Seamus was taking his own good time walking back with the ball and I watched Mr. Ahearn with some critical interest.

Suddenly Mr. Ahearn stopped and swayed a bit. I could hear the splintering of wood as the blackthorn stick split and twisted in half under his weight. Years of service had made the old stick brittle, I guess, and it could no longer bear even the weight of its elven owner.

Anyway, the stick split in half and Mr. Ahearn went down in a sort of heap. The cloth bag fell and a few cans rolled out of it. He lay in a wriggling jumble trying to get up.

We all stood transfixed for an instant. Then Kevin ran

145

over to him and hollered for me and Danny to come quick.

When Danny and I reached Mr. Ahearn we could see that he had struck his head on the sidewalk when he had fallen and that a thin trickle of blood leaked from his yellowish forehead and ran down into a busy grey eyebrow.

"Cor! Mr. Ahearn! Are ye all right?" Kevin almost shouted at the supine figure who was trying vainly to lift himself.

I had never seen Mr. Ahearn up close before. I was amazed that Kevin was touching him. He was trying to get his hands under Mr. Ahearn's arms to lift him to a sitting position. Mr. Ahearn was regaining his senses and gave Kev a little assistance. Soon he was sitting up with Kevin holding him, shaking his head to "clear the cobwebs," as Tommy used to say when he boxed in tournaments.

"Dan-o!" Kevin commanded, "Go get some ice an' a cup o' water from our fridge."

Danny took off like a shot. We were right in front of our apartment and Danny could take the stairs three at a time to our third-floor flat.

"Don't fret none, Mr. Ahearn," I heard myself saying, "Dan-o's a quick runner an' he'll get ye some water to make ye feel better."

A bit of saliva dribbled from the corner of Mr. Ahearn's mouth and I wiped it gently with the corner of my shirt. The rest of the "gang" gathered around us watching the ministerings that Kevin was directing. Danny returned with the water and a chunk of ice. Kev had Danny hold the ice against the cut on Mr. Ahearn's forehead, and he held the glass of water for Mr. Ahearn to sip.

Mr. Ahearn's vitality returned slowly.

"I thankee, boys," he said. He pronounced "boys" as "buys," but we all knew what he meant. "I guess t'auld black-thorn's give me all the service in it!"

When he could stand up, Kevin and Danny helped him by holding on to his arms and walking slowly along towards his house. I was told to carry the shopping bag, which was fairly heavy. I had retrieved the cans which had fallen out

146

and put them in the bag with the rest of the groceries. The rest of our friends watched with a vague fascination as we bundled the aged "Dallahan" off to his house. I think I watched myself and my brothers with the same fascination, hardly believing that we were doing the unthinkable.

Kevin and Danny helped Mr. Ahearn up the steps and into the old house. He hadn't locked the door when he left for the grocer's. I noticed that the place was very badly in need of paint and that the floorboards on the large front porch, which spanned the entire front of the house, were very rotten and flexed under our weight. I hoped that I wouldn't fall through to the basement.

Inside the house I stood in awe. It was dark, to be sure, but one could easily see that the house was very well kept and was as clean as any Mama would have worked in.

We had entered into a very large foyer or hall. Rooms opened off either side of this space. The foyer itself was warm and friendly in spite of its darkness. We were standing on a thick carpet with colorful designs swirled on it. The carpet was basically a very light tan or beige and the designs were in brilliant reds and blues, which we could clearly see in the light streaming in through the open door. The carpet very nearly covered a multicolored marble floor which I now know as parquet. A massive table stood against a wall and a stand next to the table held a collection of umbrellas and walking sticks. Mr. Ahearn guided Kev and Danny directly to this area, picked another blackthorn from the stand, and indicated that my brothers should release him.

"Thankee, boys," he said again. This time there was a little life in his voice. I think I expected him to croak or to have a gravelly sort of way of speaking. As it was, he had a soft voice and a thick brogue much like that of my uncles who came from Ireland.

Kev and Danny said that it was O.K. and started towards the door. Mr. Ahearn stopped them.

"A minute, Buckos. I've naught to give ye in coin for totin' an auld man home, but wait here an instant." He shuffled off into one of the rooms off of the foyer. We stood

147

and looked at each other.

"We can't take anything from Mr. Ahearn for bringin' him home, Kevin," Danny protested.

"I know, Dan-o," Kev replied, "but we can tell him when he gets back. Cor! What a place this is inside!"

We looked up and noticed a crystal chandelier above our heads. It was not extremely large but the sunlight from the door made tiny rainbows dance on the flecked wallpaper.

"Ah! Here we be, now." Mr. Ahearn thumped back into the foyer with a small box in his hand.

"Mr. Ahearn," Kevin began, "we can't take anything for . . ."

"Tush! 'Tis nothin' of value. Just an auld man's thanks for a kindness and ye've no right to deprive me of this."

Kev seemed ready to protest again, but Mr. Ahearn went on.

"You'll be Patricks. I can tell by your black hair and your mother's looks. Ye'll be the last three. This small gift is a to-ken of the Arans, where her family comes from. 'Tis carved from a ship's timbers right on the Isle of Inishmaan where the O'Hickeys are from . . . those who fled to the Isles." He opened the box. In it lay a small cross carved out of dark wood. The cross was surmounted by a circle which cut through the top, the crossbar, and beneath, as well. Instead of a Christ, the cross carried a beautiful and graceful scroll-work design carved with infinite patience. The scroll crossed over and under itself and virtually glowed with a warmth put in it by the carver.

"Cor! Mr. Ahearn, we thank you for this," Kevin gasped. "It's a real beauty."

Kevin handed the box to Danny, who looked silently and who then passed it to me. It was heavy and solid looking, yet as delicate as a flower in its beauty.

"Go on, now! Get back to your game. Auld Ahearn's got to get to his prayers and the other important things in life. Thankee again, me bucks, and tell your dear mother auld Ahearn is thankful for the Patricks this day!"

He shooed us out of his house and we went wonderingly

back to the gang, who questioned us mercilessly about the haunted house.

"Mr. Ahearn is O.K.," Kevin told them. "So don't say naught about haunts to me."

He didn't tell them anything about the house and we took that as our cue to be silent as well.

Mama was enthralled by the cross that Mr. Coleman Ahearn had given us. She said it was a Celtic cross and that, in Ireland, there are many crosses with the circle carved out of rough stones and sitting on the side of roads. She even showed the cross to Mrs. O'Malley, who had lived in the neighborhood even longer than we had.

"Auld Ahearn is a funny sort," she told Mama. "A lonely man but lonely by choice. Had a sister, he did, and they lived in the auld house long before I can remember. Never seemed to need to work or anything. . . . The sister, Maureen, was friendly enough but never went out unless she had to. She took the consumption and auld Coleman nursed her until the end. He's pleasant and gives me a nod when I see him at the shoppin', but that's all."

Kevin, my practical joker brother, had a compassionate side which marks him even to this day a half-century later. The next time he saw Mr. Ahearn trudging to the grocer with his new blackthorn stick and cloth bag, Kev trotted over to him and walked with him. When the shopping was over, the two walked back to Mr. Ahearn's house. Kevin was carrying the heavy bag.

This went on for several months. Then, abruptly, Mr. Ahearn seemed to have disappeared from the face of the Earth. The solitary light which could occasionally be seen glowing through the curtained front window was not seen anymore. I asked Kev about Mr. Ahearn.

"Don't know, Seán-o. I think I'll be askin' after him. I went and knocked yesterday but got no answer. Maybe Monsignor Hanratty knows."

Monsignor Hanratty told Kev that he, indeed, knew Mr. Ahearn well. He confided that he took him Communion occasionally and that this had gone on for years.

149

"I took him to the hospital last week. He'd been layin' up sick and needed to be out of that house. I didn't know you boys knew him . . . he kept so much to himself and his things."

Kev told him about the stickball game and about the shopping trips.

"Ah. Well, Kevin, there'll be no more shoppin' trips. Mr. Ahearn has gone to his reward. I buried him quietly the day after he died . . . Wednesday, it was. Wanted it that way, he did. There's a sister who'll be comin' from Boston to close up the house any day now."

Kev felt a bit sad that he hadn't been able to do more for this gentle man, but accepted the death and told us about it. We felt that we, at least, had been able to break through a bit of the mystery about our neighborhood "Dallahan" and dispel the darkness.

On the next weekend an ancient lady laboriously climbed the three flights to our apartment and knocked on our door. Tommy let her in. She was nicely dressed and had penetratingly blue eyes . . . much the same as those I had seen beneath Mr. Ahearn's bushy eyebrows. She introduced herself as Flore (not Flora) Feighan, Mr. Ahearn's sister.

"Coleman wanted to be alone and I honored that," she told Mama as she sat at our oilcloth-covered kitchen table sipping tea from a mug. "We wrote to each other and I sent him a bit each month to keep himself fit. He had cared well for Maureen and then lived his last years as he wanted. He kept the family home and kept it well. All of father's treasures and remembrances from the old country were kept as if in a shrine." She handed us a book, leather-covered and cracked with age. It appeared to be some sort of a ledger or diary.

"This was Maureen's book," she told us as she opened the pages of the book lying on the kitchen table, "then, after she died it became Coleman's cause."

The pages were filled with names and dates. Occasionally, there would be a small notation written in a fine hand.

150

As she moved slowly through the pages we could see where different inks and pens had been used as the years moved on.

"Maureen and Coleman had some idea that they were chosen not only to preserve the past by caring for things, but they were also to care for people by reminding God of them. Look, here's the first notation about your family!"

There, in a very fine hand, was a faded notation: 11 November 1931; Patrick, Thomas and Kathleen (Inishmaan and Kilkenny); 7350 Maxwell St. #302.

She rapidly advanced a page or so.

"And here . . . 3 March 1932; to Thomas and Kathleen Patrick—Thomas, Jr."

Each of us was noted on our birthday. I was sandwiched between "Callahan, Gerald ('Bloke' to us)," and "O'Donnell, Seamus."

Many of the earlier names had second dates marked after them which indicated the date of their passing to a better life.

"Spent his time, like Maureen, prayin' for the people he felt that God wanted him to pray for. Not much of a life, but it was the one he chose."

"How did he ever know about all of us?" Danny wanted to know.

"He had his ways. Monsignor Hanratty would tell him. He'd hear a word or two at the store. Sometimes just sittin' by his window and listenin' was enough to update him. He had his ways."

Mrs. Flore Feighan rose to leave. She said that she had hired some men to carefully pack the heirlooms Mr. Ahearn had so faithfully guarded and that they would be sent to her home in Boston. She would sell the house, which would probably be torn down to make room for a small commercial building. She tucked the old book carefully under her arm as she rose and lifted a paper-wrapped package from her lap. We hadn't even noticed that she had it when she had come in.

"Here, Mrs. Patrick, is a remembrance Coleman had set aside for you and your family. I found it with this note on it

151

on the table by the front window."

The package was not large and was wrapped in brown paper. A small square of white paper was pinned to the wrapping. The cramped writing said only: "Please give this to the Patricks, 7350 Maxwell St. #302. For their kindnesses and Kevin's assistance. It is from Kilkenny."

Mama opened the package. It was a tablecloth made of the finest Irish linen. It may have been white originally, but now it was a rich bone color. The linen was finely woven and seemed very thick for a single layer of cloth. The border was embroidered with the same fine linen thread in the curling patterns we had seen on the Celtic cross Mr. Ahearn had given us. Mama showed her appreciation for the gift and her awareness of its value with the loving gaze she cast on it.

"I'll be gone now, Mrs. Patrick. Thank you, boys, for the attention given my brother in his last days. I know that he's blessin' you from a better place." And she left.

We watched the men load boxes and furniture into a large moving truck and then all of Mr. Ahearn was gone. The tablecloth was carefully folded, wrapped in tissue, and placed in a drawer in Mama's room. I believe that Tommy has it now.

"Dan-o?" I nudged my brother under the covers on our bed that night.

"What, Seán-o?" he muttered, used to my breaking into the first waves of his sleep with some question or other.

"Mr. Ahearn was no Dallahan!" I stated emphatically.

"Nor a leprechaun, nor even a Cluricaun . . ."

"Not even a Far Darrig! He was just a nice man an' I'm going to pray for him tonight."

I did. I do. Now, many years later, I believe that this gnarled old Irishman is still praying for the Patricks, because we seem to sense it.

Danny rolled over and covered his head with the blanket, his signal that the conversation was over for the night.

"'Night, Seán-o."

"'Night, Danny . . ."

Goodnight Mr. Ahearn. Goodnight world. Goodnight God. . . .

No, Mr. Ahearn was no spirit, ghost, or Irish fairy. He was certainly no "Far Darrig," which is a nasty little creature who wears a red hat and red jacket and plays cruel tricks on people. Mr. Ahearn was none of those. But, now . . . Mr. Conneely . . .?

Kid Patrick

THE NORMAL IRISHMAN considers himself to be among the burliest of men. I really believe that, instead of walking, an Irish lad between the ages of about twenty and thirty swaggers from spot to spot. He walks with a measured tread, feet planted flatly on the pavement or floor in front of him. His shoulders pivot from side to side and his head is usually held at a jaunty angle with the chin slightly protruding and the eyelids at half-mast. His hands are invariably thrust in his trouser pockets.

Maybe I'm stereotyping, but I really believe it. At least that's the way I remember my uncles and the brawny railroaders who peopled the neighborhood I grew up in a half-century ago.

Our particular northern city was comprised of ethnic pockets. We had, besides the Irish, a goodly number of Italians, Polish, Middle Europeans, and Jews. The blacks (who were called "Coloreds" in those days) also had their section of town and we rarely saw them except on our infrequent excursions to the downtown section or on the public transportation which we all shared.

The Jews were clearly divided into two distinct classifications: the professionals, who were lawyers, doctors, and other persons of high calling; and the "rest," who were usually local merchants and who shared the same poverty . . . or near poverty . . . as the Irish and Italians.

Catholic parishes, like the city, were also ethnically divided. The Irish "had" certain parishes which were predominantly Irish, the Italians had theirs, the Polish, and so on.

St. Columbkille, for instance, was almost solidly Irish. Even the bishop must have recognized this because the pastor of St. Columbkille and his six assistants were usually full-blooded Irishmen. Our Lady of Mount Carmel and St. Rocco were led by such ethnic clergy as Msgr. Di Franco and

Father Scippione, while St. Vitus, St. Wladimir and Sts. Cyril and Methodious had priests named Olsavskey, Raszkiewicz and Evanowski.

Each parish, and especially the schools, catered to this ethnicity. St. Columbkille, for example, taught Irish history and the non-Irish in the school would learn as much about St. Brendan, St. Killian, and Eamon DeValera as the St. Roccoians would about St. Januarius' blood and Victor Emmanuel.

The one common bond we shared was the CYO Athletic League. The CYO, in our city, was massive to say the least. All of the parochial schools, with the single exception of the two Eastern Rite Catholic churches, St. Maron and St. Sava, were very large and each boasted a football team, a basketball team, and a squad of pretty-legged cheerleaders. We competed with a ferocity which would rival the American League, the National League, the NFL, the AFL, and the U.S. Olympic teams combined. The CYO championship games at the end of the various seasons were treated much the same as the adult world would treat the World Series or the Super Bowl.

To the victor belonged the spoils!

An integral sporting event in the CYO world was the annual boxing tournament. It was much the same as the famed Golden Gloves, but accommodated kids from sixth grade through twelfth. The tournament was held in the late spring of the year and commanded a good deal of publicity, both in the Diocesan and the local secular newspapers. We even had occasional short comments on the local radio news from time to time.

I attempted to follow in my brothers' footsteps in this endeavor like I did in football and basketball. After all, I made the football team; I made the basketball team, and did fairly well at that; and I was not a bad baseball player at all.

In boxing, however, survival triumphed and I was saved from having to become the Great White Hope by compassionate siblings who realized that Seán-o was not true material for the canvas ring.

155

Tommy and Billy were good boxers. They had several trophies to prove it, and Billy was the champion of the whole league in seventh grade.

Danny, my next older brother, was even pretty good. Not great, mind you, but pretty good. His "great" fight took place when he was in the ninth grade and beat the bejabbers out of Mario Ilacqua from Our Lady of Mount Carmel.

Mario was touted as "King of the Ring" by his supporters and he was very good. The problem was that he was kind of slow and Danny was wiry and quick. Dan-o danced around the ring popping little jabs that Mario didn't even see coming. He landed a lot of points right in the first round. Mario was so flustered at having this little freckled Irishman snapping leather off his nose that he lost his calm, deliberate delivery and became an uncoordinated windmill, swinging at the air around him.

Danny was never a class champion, but he did hold his own very well and I was always proud to be in his corner to hand him his towel and to give him my words of advice and encouragement.

Kevin was the real boxer. He, like Tommy and Billy, was a "natural" at almost any athletic venture he cared to pursue. He had a very nice physical build and suppleness which made his body adaptable to the rigors of training for a sport and he soon developed muscle tone and all those things of which true athletes are made.

I think that the thing that really made the difference, though, was the fact that Kev genuinely enjoyed the thrill of competition. Just as he was a modest and happy winner, he was also a good loser. He was never on a "downer" because of a loss or a bad game, as far as I can remember. It can truly be said that Kevin lived for the game rather than the laurels.

Kev trained hard for all of his sports. He obeyed training rules religiously and kept himself physically fit out of sheer desire to be able to compete and enjoy his sports. This also motivated him in his academics, because one had to keep a certain average in school in order to be counted as a member of one of the many athletic teams. Kev studied hard so that his grades would keep him suited up. His diligence always seemed to pay off.

Like Tommy, Billy, and David before him, Kevin began boxing in the sixth grade. He did quite well and earned several trophies while he was still at St. Columbkille. He was well known around the school and even the parish. It was not uncommon for adults to slap Kevin on the shoulder as we left the church after Sunday Mass and comment on his latest triumph.

I think that the one accolade which pleased Kevin most came in his eighth-grade year when, after pounding his way to triumph over his opponents in the boxing tournament, Father Killeen announced from the pulpit that "Kid Patrick, right there in the second pew with his family, added his name to those of such Irish greats as Dempsey and Tunney . . . and, indeed, John L. Sullivan . . . in the CYO tournament last evening!"

Our parish was lavish with superlatives, but we wouldn't have dreamt of contradicting them!

When Kev was in the tenth grade he trained in real earnest for the tournament. Billy and Danny were also competing in their respective divisions. Tommy was out of school and, hence, out of the CYO. David and I had seen the wisdom of being in our brothers' corners rather than in the ring itself.

Tommy, David, and I were active as "managers" and "trainers" for our active participants. We would trot alongside of them as they jogged the cluttered streets of our neighborhood, hold towels for them or pass spit buckets while they rested between rounds, and massage tight muscles after a lengthy workout.

Kevin rose early every day and ran around the neighborhood before it even began to get light. He did all sorts of exercises and drank too much milk. During this time, it was not uncommon for him to be in bed and asleep before Danny and I even crawled into our bed. Kevin, being older, had the privilege of a half-hour later bedtime than Danny and I, but chose to forego that for the sleep his young body

157

required to prepare it for the rigors of athletic competition.

At fifteen, Kevin was about five foot seven and weighed in at a trim 140 pounds. His shoulders were broad and his waist waspish. His musculature was not spectacular, but even an untrained eye could see that he was "hard" and had no flab. His body movements were fluid and easy. Kev had a grace of movement which told much to athletic observers and which paid off in large dividends in the boxing ring.

The competition in Kev's tenth-grade tournament was not really too fantastic, and Kevin was thought to be an easy victor. He never listened to these stories, though, and trained as though he would be competing for the World Heavyweight Crown against the Brown Bomber (Joe Louis) himself.

After his daily workout in St. Columbkille's gym, Kev would shower and flop on a table so that David and I could knead his legs and shoulders to loosen up the knotted muscles. At this time he would usually start a non-stop chain of chatter about his feelings regarding the upcoming tournament.

"You know, David," he would say, "McCrory from St. Bridget's is no pushover. He's got a left hook that comes like lightning from nowhere. Then, there's Pisano from over at St. Rocco. That little guy is all over the ring. If I draw one of them early on there's no tellin' what'll happen. OUCH! Seán-o! That's me leg you're diggin' your fingers in!"

The tournament lasted one solid week. Life—and school—went on as usual but without the grimness of the daily grind, because even the teachers were great fans of the Big Event.

Each winning fighter would box three times and the ultimate winners would compete in the finals on Saturday evening. The tournament was always held at Loyola High School, the Jesuit boys' school on the far side of town. We all saved streetcar fare from our various jobs so that we would be able to get there. Mama flatly refused to attend, saying that she saw no sense watching her very own boys acting like animals. She had little patience with any sport which didn't

158

involve throwing, hitting, or kicking a ball.

The crosstown ride to Loyola took about forty minutes on the old streetcar and St. Columbkille supporters usually filled several cars before the evening was over. About midway we would meet up with kids and parents from St. Vitus, which was on the same line as we were. The rides were part of the fun because there was a lot of good-natured banter between the competing schools and a warm feeling of rivalry even among the parents.

On arrival at Loyola, the fighters would strip down to the altogether and stand in a long line for a cursory examination by the doctor who was donating his time for the event. Tommy, David, and I stood alongside our brothers, holding their clothing, our threadbare towels, and the family bucket which would be in the Patrick corner during the fight.

Once examined and passed, they could "suit up" and saunter around the locker room sparring with themselves in a mirror or sitting silently in what I supposed was mental preparation for their event.

Kev did remarkably well in his first fight. He did draw Mario Pisano (he was the boy who was all over the ring), and neatly outboxed St. Rocco's finest from the beginning of the very first round.

By round three, Kevin had scored enough points that it was a virtual walk-away. Mario even apparently conceded and was spending his energy trying to avoid Kevin's prancing stride as my brother snapped hurtful little jabs off of his opponent's safety helmet and jaw.

When Kevin was announced as winner there was a huge cheer from the fathers and boys who populated the large high school gym. Kev raised his right arm and danced his little jig to show that he acknowledged the applause directed his way and that he appreciated the recognition. Mario came over to Kevin and hugged him to show that he was a good sport about the whole thing.

We were very late getting home from the fight and I had a hard time getting up for school the next day. I did, though, and was glad to be there because everyone was talking about

Kevin's easy win and I was proud that I was identified with him.

"Cor, Seán-o!" Bloke was enthusiastically saying to me, "Kev really mauled that Eye-talian boy from the first bell, didn't he?"

Bloke hadn't done too badly himself in the 110-pound class. He had neatly tucked away Regis O'Sullivan from St. Bridget's and looked very promising for the rest of the week.

Kevin's second match of the tournament was with a young Irishman from the St. Gregory the Great CYO. His name was Francie Foley and he was the younger brother of one Owen Foley, who had been the heavyweight champion about six years prior. Francie had a good reputation and I remembered him from his first bout. He had won an easy victory over a guy named Joseph who had a Polish last name with about two hundred consonants and no vowels. When we had gone to the locker room with Kevin after his bout, Francie had been on the rubbing table and former champion Owen was massaging his shoulders and telling him what he should have done. I had thought that he had done very well, indeed.

Francie was a bit taller than Kevin and not as well proportioned. He was quick, though, and had a flair of being able to make his opponent move around quite a bit in order to throw a punch at him. He had blondish-red hair and a lot of freckles. He wore blue trunks, which were St. Gregory the Great's color. We St. Columbkillians wore traditional Irish green and gold.

We went through the whole routine of examination, shadow boxing, getting hands taped, and the like the night of Kev's second bout. Kevin was loose and very much at ease. He seemed to thrive on the prospect of physical competition. He joked easily with Billy as I went out with David and Tommy to watch Danny win over his opponent from St. Vitus.

After Danny's bout I went back to the locker room to report that the crowd was even greater than it had been on the first night and that St. Columbkille had probably the largest contingent of parents present because of the cheers that Danny had gotten. Kev seemed pleased but otherwise unaffected by my announcement. Francie Foley was seated on the rubbing table listening intently to his brother Owen, who was obviously giving him some last-minute advice. Earlier fighters, the lower weight classes, were showering or dressing and, in general, just milling around.

Both Kevin and Francie were given rousing ovations when they were introduced. Kev danced a little, which told me that he was a bit nervous as he waited for the bell to sound.

At the bell, Kevin moved easily towards center ring and met Francie with a barrage of quick little jabs. Francie countered with some jabs of his own, and the two settled down to the business of taking each other's measure. Most of the round was spent this way, with neither gaining a distinct advantage over the other.

The bell sounded to end the round and Kev sank down on the stool in the Patrick corner for the ministrations of his crew.

"He leans forward when he jabs," Kevin said to Tommy.

"I noticed that, too. You might," Tommy said, "give the boy-o the auld Patrick Combo and see if that shakes him at all."

The Patrick Combo was a succession of punches that Tommy and Billy had both used very effectively. Kevin relied on his own ingenuity and didn't put too much stock in the material developed by others.

What it was, in effect, was a series of about three very quick and subtle jabs followed by a mean right cross. If the cross landed, the Patrick was expected to follow instantly with a vicious left jab thrown from the shoulder and then another right. Not very scientific, tremendously complicated to try to remember when someone was punching at you, but copywritten and tested by at least two semi-successful Patricks before Kevin.

"I might at that. . . ." Kevin mused as the bell sounded for round two.

The round wasn't even a minute old when Kevin found his opportunity to try the Patrick Combo. He saw his opening and popped three lightning-quick jabs on Francie's chin like a typewriter.

The jabs must've stunned Francie because his guard dropped for an instant. Kev's right arced out and caught Francie half on the earpiece of the helmet and half on the jaw. His rubber mouthguard sailed out of the ring.

The trouble with the Patrick Combo was that it was almost impossible to stop the sequence once it was started. The right hook was followed automatically by the tremendous left jab, which caught Francie full in the face, and the clobbering right which followed sent him flying across the ring against the ropes.

The ropes held Francie up for an instant but, like cabbage in the frying pan, he quickly wilted and sank to the canvas in a heap. Blood was gushing from his pulverized nose and lips. He was out like a lightbulb.

All eyes were on Francie as his seconds rushed into the ring to help him. They got him back to his corner and he was soon groggily shaking his head and looking at the bloody towel that Owen was pressing on and off his face.

I turned to look at Kevin. Instead of seeing my brother bouncing on his toes with the adrenaline of the fight, I saw him standing stock still with his arms hanging limply at his sides. The color had gone out of his face and he stared at Francie with uncomprehending eyes which were filled with tears.

The referee ended the bout and declared Kevin the winner "by a knockout in the second round!" Kevin showered and he, David, Danny, and I went home.

We had been home almost an hour when Tommy and Billy arrived.

"You've drawn Mulrennan from St. Bridget's for the championship!" Billy told Kev.

"It's over, Bill," Kevin said quietly. "No more for me."

"You're not backin' out, are ye?" Billy and Tommy seemed stunned.

162

"You're a cinch to take Mulrennan!" Tommy said.

"It's over!"

Kevin turned abruptly and went to the bedroom, leaving his stunned brothers to stand and watch him. We left him alone for a long while before we went to the bedroom ourselves.

"Kev," Tommy said when we were getting undressed for bed. "I think I know what you're meanin'."

Kevin was already in bed with his head turned to the wall. Danny was sitting on the edge of our bed, so I went and sat next to him.

"It's too much, Tommy. I saw his face and saw his blood. There's no sport in that for me."

"You're your own man, Kev," Tommy said quietly. He went over to David and Kevin's bed and lightly touched Kevin's shoulder.

"I just don't see me makin' someone hurt so bad . . ."

"I love ya, Kevin," came out of my mouth.

"You're really a champ, brother!" Danny said.

Kevin didn't fight again. He confined his athletic prowess to football, basketball, and track, and excelled in all three. He took a lot of "knocks" about his backing out of the tournament, but stood up to them like the young man he was.

After Danny, Kevin was very close to me and I loved him very much. I never realized it as much as I did that night when he "backed out" of the competition.

"Kev?"

"What, Seán-o?"

"Did it hurt when he hit ye?"

"He had a good punch, Seán-o."

"Quiet an' go to sleep!" came from Danny.

"'Night, guys."

"Kev?"

"What, Seán-o?"

"I love ye."

"You said that!"

"I know. 'Night."

"GOOD-NIGHT, SEÁN-O!"

163

Conneely

CORBIN CONNEELY WAS SELDOM SEEN outside of St. Columbkille church, except for infrequent excursions to the local grocer's or an occasional (very occasional) stop at the Shamrock Pub.

On the very rare instances when he did stop in the Shamrock, it was to imbibe several pints of beer liberally fortified by half-bottles of Guinness' Stout. Mr. Conneely would drink an inch or so of the frothy beer and then take the bottle of Stout at his elbow and pour some in the beer until the glass was full.

He would then lift the mixture to his lips and drink the whole thing down without so much as a breath during the process. He would sit for a moment and then start the whole thing over again until several pints had been quaffed, with only the few necessary words to the bartender spoken to order his refills.

We Patricks saw a lot more of Mr. Conneely than most of the neighborhood because we were the early Mass servers for many years. Sister Saint Bridget must have thought that a Patrick came with a built-in alarm clock, because she scheduled one of us for the 5:45 Mass during the week and the 6 A.M. Mass on Sunday with very few exceptions.

Moments before Mass would begin Mr. Conneely would tread in much like a stalker surveying his domain and looking out for any poachers in his territory. He would pause at the front pew on the Gospel side and bow deeply. Then, he would genuflect slowly and rise. The bow was repeated and only then would he enter the pew and kneel in a half-sitting fashion with his long arms stretched out in front of him and his head bent to a resting position on them. Day after day after day after day. . . .

Mr. Conneely lived in one of the few houses in our neighborhood. It was a very tiny frame house scrunched between two imposing and decaying four-story apartments much

164

like ours. The weathered siding had acquired the tint of silver as the wood, unpainted for many eons, had bared itself and become one with the elements. It did have a real slate roof, though, and occasionally a shingle would fall to the pavement on the side of the house and splinter into a dozen pieces, which would be quickly gathered by some neighborhood urchin and distributed as hopscotch markers or—if the piece was large enough—for a skipping stone when we went to the lagoon. Slate could be made to do three or four good "hops" if thrown over the water with care and skill.

"He's an Inishmaaner," Mama patiently explained when we talked of the eccentricities of Mr. Conneely. "They keep to themselves and mind their own business."

Mama explained that an "Inishmaaner" was a person from one of the three Aran Isles off the western coast of Ireland.

"There are three islands there, just off the coast of Galway Bay. Inishmore . . . that's the big island, Inishmaan and Inisheer. The people who live there have very hard lives and they must work very diligently to exist," she told us. "Fishin', mainly, though some do crafts and knittin' of the sweaters and scarves. Kevin, that beautiful white sweater you're wearin' now is from the Arans, as I'm sure you recall."

Mama went on to tell of a distant uncle of hers who was the lightkeeper on the farthest and smallest of the island chain. He dwelt in solitary splendor on Eeargh Isle and saved thousands of vessels from imminent doom by tending the lighthouse for many years.

Little by little, bit by bit, we slowly learned much about Mr. Corbin Conneely. Like many Irishmen, he waited until late to consider marrying. The girl he had chosen (without the formality of letting her know that he was interested in her) went and married another suitor and Mr. Conneely was left to start afresh.

Eventually, Mr. Conneely came to the United States and got a job on the fishing boats in New England. An injury caused him to "retire" on a small pension and he moved to our city, where he had a sister whose husband owned a tiny grocery. He didn't live with them, though, as his savings were sufficient for him to buy his very small house and give him the solitude that he undoubtedly needed to maintain his status as an Inishmaaner.

One day in the early fall something happened to him that would alter our lives a bit.

It was a cold, drizzly, rainy, very uncomfortable day. As usual (a Patrick always drew the Early Mass assignment on days like that!), Danny and I were serving Father Gilhooley's 5:45 Mass. I had the job of toting the gooseneck lamp around so that the ancient Shepherd of Souls could see the book to read the prayers. Danny half-dozed and only muttered the Latin responses as we both staggered through the ageless ritual in the overheated church.

Mr. Conneely was in his usual position and in his usual posture. His head rested flatly on his outstretched arms and his rear end rested equally as flatly on the edge of the pew seat behind him. He was either praying very devoutly or sleeping very soundly, I reasoned.

Mr. Conneely rose from his pew to take Communion when the time came. When he returned to his pew, however, he sat down, which was very much out of character for him. The only time we had ever seen him actually sit in church was during the sermon at the Sunday Mass.

He sat like he knelt, flatly. He also leaned heavily on the oak side of the pew.

When Mass was over Danny and I went about the routine business of cleaning up. I put out the candles and Danny got the cruets of wine and water to prepare them for the seven o'clock Mass which would be said by Father O'Toole or Father O'Reilly. Father Gilhooley, after considerable wandering around the sacristy, found his kneeling bench and collapsed on it to pray for the world and the parishioners of St. Columbkille.

I dawdled around after I put the candles out and made a big show out of resetting the huge ribbon markers in the Altar Missal. I liked to look at the sacred book and felt a certain pride in the fact that I could usually get the markers in the right place for the next Mass. After all, the Missal was totally in Latin.

As I turned to leave the sanctuary, I noticed that Mr. Conneely hadn't moved from his seat. Usually he was up and gone just as soon as the priest had exited the altar. This time he was just sitting there . . . or slumping there. His head rolled slightly and I thought that I could hear him breathing very loudly. I ran into the sacristy.

"Dan-o!" I called to my brother. It was loud enough for even the hard-of-hearing Father Gilhooley to lift his head for an instant.

"Dan-o! You better come an' look. Mr. Conneely's awful strange out in the church!"

Danny followed me and we went to the pew where Mr. Conneely was still slumping. Danny shook him by the shoulder. There was no response other than a faint groan. I could see that his half-open eyes were staring vacantly.

"Cor! Seán-o! We'd better get a priest or someone. I think the bugger's dyin' right here!"

Danny turned and ran back to the sacristy. I started to follow but figured that someone ought to stay with Mr. Conneely. I guessed that I was elected.

"'sO.K., Mr. Conneely," I intoned softly, "Dan-o's gettin' help fer ye. Don't fret none, Dan-o's a quick runner an' he'll get someone here before ye know it!"

I realized that I had rested my hand on Mr. Conneely's shoulder as a sort of reassurance for him. His head continued its pendulum-like swaying. Saliva drooled out of a corner of his mouth. I wiped it with the corner of my jacket.

Father O'Toole arrived in a trot with his partially buttoned cassock flying around his legs. Danny followed him and I noticed that he hadn't even removed his wool stocking hat.

"It looks like a stroke!" Father O'Toole was saying. "Danny, run to the rectory and tell the housekeeper to call the police quick. Seán-o, get a candle from the altar so I can give him the Last Rites."

"Take your HAT OFF!" I hissed at Danny as he turned to leave. He either ignored me or didn't hear me. I ran up the steps of the altar and got one of the large candles. Father O'Toole had disappeared into the sacristy and hurried back out with some small gold containers—the holy oils for Extreme Unction.

I didn't understand the Latin prayers that Father O'Toole intoned, but I figured they were asking God to help His servant make the passage from this world to the next. I stood respectfully by holding the lighted candle as the priest annointed Mr. Conneely with the oils and said many prayers over him.

Danny had returned and was standing next to me watching. He still had his hat on.

"Cor, Dan-o!" I hissed again, "Take your hat off, will ye?"

This time he heard me and quickly snatched the blue stocking cap off of his head. Father O'Toole also heard me because he looked up impatiently at the interruption. It was only momentary annoyance, however, because he went right back to his business of getting Mr. Conneely's soul ready for its journey to Heaven.

Pat and Tony arrived as Father O'Toole was finishing the Last Rites. They manhandled Mr. Conneely out of the pew and carried him bodily out to their police car to rush him to the Saint Vincent. The siren wailed to life as they pulled away from the curb and headed down Hardin Street. Tony was driving and Pat was in the back seat holding on to Mr. Conneely.

Fortunately for Mr. Conneely, his stroke was termed a "mild" one. From my viewpoint it looked for all the world like about the worst sickness I had ever seen in my thirteen years. But he was soon out of the Saint Vincent and back in his small house.

It was necessary for him to have a nurse with him for a considerable time because the stroke had left him partially paralyzed and only time would get all the parts working in good order again. The nurse was a formidable woman who was strong enough to handle the most obstinant male patient.

168

Her name was Mrs. Flynn. She was a widow and Mama said that she was about forty-five years old. She ruled Mr. Conneely with an iron fist and took no nonsense from any of her patients.

Mama liked to send a meal down to Mr. Conneely from time to time during his convalescence. She felt that Mrs. Flynn had enough to do taking care of him, and didn't have much time to prepare nourishing meals. Furthermore, she believed that they both could use the moral support a good bit of cod or a nice hot chowder would bring.

I was—am—naturally nosy and I used to like to be the one asked to deliver the offerings to the Conneely household. That meant that I would get inside and see what was going on. Then, of course, I felt duty-bound to report my findings to the family-at-large.

Mr. Conneely improved steadily. He walked with a cane for a time but this was soon discarded. Mrs. Flynn was soon relegated to only coming a few days a week. In time, Mr. Conneely was almost as good as new.

One fringe benefit of the whole experience was the chance to hear Mr. Conneely talk about his life on Inishmaan. Danny and I spent a goodly amount of our time during his illness listening to him tell of his life as a fisherman, about the island and, especially, about the beauty of the ruins of Dun Conor which were on his island.

Mrs. Flynn encouraged his storytelling because it was good for him to practice his speech, which had been hampered by the stroke.

"The people from the Muir Ara (Sea of Aran) are fine indeed, but it takes gettin' to know 'em." Mama explained.

One evening in the late spring Kevin trotted into the apartment with a message for Danny and me.

"I was passin' by auld Conneely's place when he called to me and made me to come in his house," Kevin said breathlessly. "He wants to see Dan-o an' Seán tomorrow if they'll stop by."

"What's it about?" Danny asked.

"I don't know, Dan-o," Kevin said, "but he seemed to

think it to be important the way he asked me."

We went after school the next afternoon on our way to Patrick's Corner to shine shoes and sell newspapers. Mr. Conneely opened the door immediately when we knocked.

"Come in, lads," he said conspiritorially. "Come in an' sit for a minute. I've an immense favor to be asking of ye."

The favor, though not immense as far as we could see, was asked. Would we, Dano-o and I, serve a special Mass on Easter Monday? It was to be at ten o'clock and Father O'Toole was to say it. We were also asked not to breathe a word to a soul—not even Mama—about the reason for the Mass.

We kept our secret well.

On Easter Monday we were at the church. Father O'Toole was vested for Mass and Danny and I put on the white cassocks with the red velvet collars and cuffs which were reserved for only very special occasions in our parish.

As part of our "promise," we had asked Mama, our brothers, and Pat and Tony to be there, as well.

Pat and Tony were on duty and arrived at the church in their police uniforms, gunbelts and all. They took their places in the front pews.

At precisely ten o'clock Father O'Toole and his two grinning Irish servers arrived at the foot of the altar. After a few moments of organ music from Mr. Bouchard, our French organist who played for literally every occasion at St. Columbkille, Mr. Conneely walked slowly from the side aisle where he had been standing unnoticed by everyone. He stood at the altar rail and waited expectantly.

The organ music swelled and Mrs. Flynn walked majestically down the center aisle holding a bouquet of daisies and small rose buds.

She was all alone, yet she smiled as though she grasped the treasure of the world in her hand.

When they stood before him, Father O'Toole leaned over and whispered to Danny and then to me. We were instructed to go out of the altar rail and stand to the right of Mr. Conneely.

"Mr. Conneely wishes to have two best men!" Father

O'Toole announced to the small assemblage.

After the wedding Mr. Conneely gave Danny a large box and instructed him to take it home to open it.

"A remembrance for all of you for your kindness to an auld Inishmaaner," he said.

When we got home we opened the box. Everyone was anxious to see what was in it.

We found three wrapped boxes in the large box. One, the largest, was tagged for "The Patrick Family." The two smaller ones were tagged, too, one for Danny and one for me.

Mama opened the larger box. It was a carved boat. It looked like a ferry, or a boat to carry people. On the side was painted the name *Naomh Eanna*.

"That's the name of the boat that carries people from Galway to the Isles," Mama told us. "Named after Saint Enda, it is. He's the saint who brought Christ to those islands."

The carving was beautiful and the grain of the wood was polished to a glowing warmth. It would sit for many years on the center of the small mantelpiece in our apartment and, after Mama was gone, in the same honored spot in Danny's home.

The two smaller packages contained identical carved replicas of Inish fishing boats, called curraghs. One was named the *Dan-o* and the other bore the name *Seán-o*. Along the sides of the boats was carved a Gaelic phrase in small, delicate letters reminiscent of the style of the Book of Kells. The words were: *Oro Se Do Bheatha Bhaile*.

"Dan-o?" I poked my brother under our common blanket.

Danny stirred and turned towards me.

"What, Seán-o? It's late."

"It was nice, bein' in the wedding."

"I liked it, too."

"Who'd have thought that Mr. Conneely would marry Mrs. Flynn?"

"I guess he didn't want to take no chances in losin'

another colleen!"

Calling Mrs. Flynn a "colleen" wasn't quite what I had expected and I giggled a little.

"I wonder what it means, the Irish on the side of our boats, Dan-o."

"I asked Mama in the kitchen," Danny said, and rolled over onto his side again.

"Well, what does it mean?" I pestered.

"She said she could only give me kind of the meaning instead of the exact words."

"What does it mean?"

"She says it means, kind of, "welcome home.""

"That's nice, Dan-o. I'm gonna keep my boat forever."

"'Night, Seán-o."

Good-night, Dan-o. Goodnight, Mr. and Mrs. Conneely. Good-night world. *Oro Se Do Bheatha Bhaile.*

The Conflagration

OUR NEIGHBORHOOD WAS NOT IMMUNE to tragedy. I guess we were very fortunate that most major calamities which could have happened, did not occur. Most of the things which did happen were of such a minor nature, in comparison with what *could* have happened, that we were blest indeed.

In retrospect, our apartment was a prime example of survival in spite of all of the obvious things working against you. The building was close to fifty years old when I lived there . . . and I stayed there for almost nineteen years. It was still standing three years ago when I went home for Mama's funeral, and people were still living in it. This was almost thirty years after I left!

I remember, especially, how tinder-dry the basement was. Each of the twelve families who inhabited the small units on the floors above had a "locker," or storage area, in the basement. This meant a large amount of wooden walls in the basement proper.

The furnace was a gigantic coal furnace with a massive "Iron Fireman" coal stoker in front of it. A dozen or so metal trash cans stood against the wooden wall of lockers and hot "clinkers" would be removed daily from the furnace and dumped unceremoniously into the cans, where they steamed, smoked and, at times, even flamed up for a goodly period of time until they cooled.

Why these circumstances alone didn't cause at least one minor fire in our apartment is, for me, absolute proof that God was watching out for us. By all of the laws of science and spontaneous combustion, we should have been a three-story towering inferno many times over.

The wiring in our building was also very haphazard. Loose wires with rotting insulation hung in garlands from the basement rafters. Fuse wire was supposed to be used (the type of fuses you screw in hadn't been invented yet) on the electrical panels for safety's sake, but oftentimes a suspicious-looking strand of regular wire could be seen peeping out from the panel on the wall in back of the huge, stationary washtubs. It was the same kind of ingenuity that later thought of putting a penny in the fuse hole, I guess.

The worst thing that ever happened to our building, at least as far back as I can remember, was when part of the wooden stairway between the first- and second-floor back porches rotted and crashed down. The landlord had the entire back end of the apartment rebuilt after that and the new back porches were the best part of the building for a long, long time. (No one was even on the stairs when they collapsed, either. They just fell of their own weight . . . no big thing.)

We did have one horrible accident at Patrick's Corner early one morning. Euclid Street was a major thoroughfare and had streetcar tracks in the middle. Every couple of blocks there was a "safety island" of cement where people could stand to wait for the streetcars. The ends of the islands were protected by huge concrete abutments which were called "stanchions." Each of these was topped off by a high lightpole.

Early one morning a large trailer truck carrying potatoes (of all things) careened down the street with the driver having apparently fallen asleep. It crashed head-on into the concrete stanchion and the trailer rolled easily over the cab of the tractor, neatly slicing the top of the cab, as well as the top of the driver, off. Danny and I were just walking over to serve the 5:45 A.M. Mass at St. Columbkille when the accident happened and we were among the first on the scene. I had never seen violent death before and got sick right there on Euclid Street. Danny helped me to church and made me drink water before we served the Mass.

I vividly remember standing on the curb watching the steam escape from the crushed truck cab and wondering if the decapitated driver felt any pain. Engine fluids and blood flowed together in long rivers which ran along the curb to the storm drain opening.

Pat and Tony were there almost right after the accident

174

happened and used their call box to summon a fire engine and an ambulance. Danny and I didn't wait around to see what else would happen because we had to serve the Mass. I do remember potatoes lying in the puddled road. It looked very incongruous and almost obscene.

As I have said, our neighborhood was very fortunate. We were certainly luckier than most. But, for each generation, it seemed, there was one event from which time could be calculated.

The event in my generation was The Fire. Even today my brothers and I will reminisce and place an event or happening at "two years before The Fire," or, " . . . just after The Fire. . . ."

This conflagration to which I refer began innocently enough on a warm June morning shortly after we began our summer vacation. I had just completed the eighth grade and was getting ready to enter Holy Redeemer High School. I also had my first "full-time" job during the summer. (I still worked at Patrick's Corner every afternoon as the Shoeshine Patrick. No getting out of a family business. But I had gotten the job of helping John the Hardware for three or four hours every morning as a kind of "stock boy.")

Anyway, I was working for John the Hardware and had just finished rolling four kegs of nails to their places behind the counter when Mrs. O'Farrell came rushing into the store hollering something about a fire in the tenement next door.

The reason she came into the hardware store was that no one in the tenement building had a phone and most of that type of business was taken care of by John the Hardware. John wore a hearing aid and Mrs. O'Farrell had to shout it a second time before John picked up the phone and dialed the fire department. John's nosy employee (me) ran out of the store and looked at the apartment next to the shop. I could see very black smoke coming down the alleyway between the tenement and us so I thought better of venturing in that direction.

People were running down the street towards the smoke

175

by now and several cars had stopped in the street. Mrs. O'Farrell came back out of the store and stood next to me, wringing her hands in her apron and looking terrified. (Mrs. O'Farrell was one of the Killarney O'Farrells who migrated, it appears, en masse from Ireland at the turn of the century. She lived alone now that her children had married, and was—like Mama—a washerwoman.)

"How did it start?" I asked Mrs. O'Farrell, who was busy trying to cry or pray or both.

"I don't know, Seán-o, I don't know. The porches started burnin' t'was when I noticed it. I think it started from the trash pile in the yard."

The smoke was much thicker by now and I could see tongues of orange flame occasionally through the smoke. The orange looked soiled and unclean. People were coming out of the building now carrying all sorts of things: piles of clothing, here a chair and, over there, a sewing machine. . . . Sirens which I hadn't noticed approaching sounded suddenly very, very loud.

Three engines from the Seventy-Third Street Station pulled up in front of the building and firemen jumped off of the still-moving trucks and went about their trade. One engine dropped a load of hose off of the back and kept rolling towards the corner. The hose unfolded as the truck moved so that, when they reached the corner where the hydrant was located, all the fireman had to do was couple on to the iron dog-potty and twist his large wrench to get a flow of water coursing along the canvas hose.

The firemen moved us away so that they could get down the alley. I ventured across the street which, by now, was devoid of moving traffic. I could see much better from here, I thought.

Danny, who was working as a vegetable boy for Hughes' Market down the street, ran up breathless. He was still wearing his soiled white apron and looked like he had no pants on since it fell far below his shorts.

"Cor! Seán-o! How did it start?"

I told him what Mrs. O'Farrell had told me and turned to

176

look at the fire again. The flames were pulsing high above the roof by this time and firemen were scampering in and out of the building. The massive hook and ladder (which Billy would drive in another year or so) had raised its high ladder to the building roof. Several other ladders were placed at windows on the doomed building's face. Firemen were climbing the ladders like acrobats with no apparent fear of falling off.

Suddenly the air split with a muffled thud which, an instant later, turned into a horrendous BLAM! Windows on the first floor exploded and glass flew every which way. Some of the firemen ran towards us shouting for us to "move, Move, MOVE!!!" We did. We ran almost a block away.

"Seán-o! You're burnin'!" Danny shouted at me. He started slapping my chest furiously.

I looked where Danny was hitting me and saw an ember of sorts glowing and flying from under Danny's pummeling hand. I guessed that it was a piece of the explosion which had gotten on my shirt. I had been too excited to notice.

I was feeling giddy. I grabbed Danny's shoulder and pulled his ear over to me and hissed, "Take your apron off. You look nekked with it wrapped about ye!"

Danny paid no attention. His eyes were riveted to the burning building. The crowd was very loud now and a collective gasp rose almost visibly.

One of the ladders had caught fire and, as a segment of the wall gave way, crashed in a shower of sparks. Two firemen had been on the ladder at that moment.

Several people still leaned out of windows on the third and fourth floors, shouting and waving for help to reach them. Then, one by one, they leapt to the pavement below. The fire was apparently too hot for the firemen, even, and there was no way for ladders or safety nets to be placed to aid the victims on the upper floors.

Several other fire trucks had arrived and a whole group of firemen had begun spraying water on the buildings on either side of the burning apartment. I stood dumbly watching and worried about my lunch and personal things that were in the hardware store. I worried about John the Hardware and what would happen to him if his store burned. I worried about the people I saw falling through space from their apartment windows to the concrete alley-way . . .

"Oh, God, Seán-o!"

Danny was holding my shirt so tightly that it was ripping under his clenched fingers. His face was all scrunched up and tears were coursing down his cheeks, making black runs on his soot-covered face.

More screams. I couldn't look anymore and I buried my own face in Danny's chest. I'm not sure which of us was shaking, or if both of us were, but we stood clenched together as violent tremors ran through us from an emotional source too deep to name.

There was a loud, muffled, tearing, crashing, thudding, whooshing noise which filled the air, followed by a massive intake of breath from the crowd. I looked up from Danny's chest and saw the last part of the apartment crumble as it collapsed in on itself. Sparks, flames, and horribly black smoke billowed in huge puffs from the caving-in ruins. I turned and ran towards home.

I was already climbing the steps to our apartment when Danny caught up with me. He was still wearing his apron. He grabbed my shorts as I climbed the stairs two at a time.

I reached the landing and turned viciously to my brother.

"You're pullin' me damned britches off!" I yelled at him and, I think, I tried to take a wild swing at him.

Danny let go of my shorts and grabbed me tightly and pulled me to him. He was still crying.

"Seán-o! Seán-o! Seán-o!" was all he kept saying. Mr. Feldman came out and helped both of us up the last flight of stairs to our own apartment. No one else was home, but we felt safe when we had gotten inside.

I felt particularly guilty because I still didn't know what had happened to the hardware store or what had become of the McHugh family—one of two families we knew

178

particularly well who lived in the destroyed building.

Nine people perished in that fire. Three of them were firemen and the other six were people whom we did not know too well. Several others were seriously injured from either burns or from their leap to safety from their apartment windows. Again, no one we knew too well.

A funeral Mass was held at St. Columbkille for seven of the victims. All of the firemen and four of the other victims had been members of that parish. The other two were Protestant and were buried from the Hardin Street Presbyterian Church on the same day.

The hardware store was damaged, but not beyond repair, and I helped clean up for several days after the ashes had cooled down. John the Hardware wanted to pay me more than my 30 cents an hour for the hard work I had to do, but I told him I didn't want any more. (Several weeks after The Fire, John the Hardware gave me my weekly pay envelope and a heavy package wrapped in brown paper and tied with twine. I opened it when I got home and found a set of screwdrivers and wrenches I had been admiring. I commented once how nice they would be for working on our bicycles. I guess John the Hardware thought that this Patrick deserved a bonus! I thanked him for it the next day I worked.)

Danny and I had to answer a thousand questions that night at supper. Everyone, Mama included, wanted to know exactly what we had seen. We eventually got kind of tired of telling and retelling the story of The Fire.

Danny and I both showered for a long time that day. It seemed to take forever for the sooty grime to wash off. It seemed to be greasy.

I had a small red mark on my chest from where the piece of burning stuff landed. It didn't hurt, though. Mama patched my t-shirt so that it could still be worn.

I slept kind of fitfully that night. Once I was jostled awake and felt Danny's face buried in my shoulder. He was crying and trying not to wake me. I turned to face him and we held each other silently until his crying stopped and we fell

179

asleep again.

Both Billy and Kevin became firemen when they were old enough and faced many, many perils in their careers. Both eventually became battalion chiefs and both were decorated for heroism several times during their years in service to the community. Kevin, in particular, was awarded a gold medal for his selfless rescue of a family of seven. He rushed in and out of the burning house several times to carry the children, shielded by his heavy coat, to safety as burning debris rained down on him. On his last trip, he had to crawl out on his hands and knees with an infant clutched tightly to his chest under his coat.

"Seán-o?" Danny said as we lay awake the following morning. All of the others were still asleep and the daylight was barely breaking through the holes in our window shade.

"What, Danny?"

"I'm gonna' pray every night that we never have a fire!" he said after a moment.

"Me, too!" I said emphatically.

"An', I'm gonna' pray for firemen and policemen, too."

"Me, too, Dan-o!" I said again.

It has been thirty-six years since The Fire. I have kept my promise and I'm sure Danny has, too.

"Dan-o," I said the other night on the phone after calling my big brother long distance for some silly reason, "do you remember when Kev let the chicken loose at Holy Redeemer?"

"Was that just before or just after The Fire?" he responded.

The Piper

THE IRISH, IN GENERAL, are very musical people. They love to sing, especially the sad songs of their Motherland, or vicious chants against Britain for usurping their liberty. When I was young I always thought of the fiddle as a genuine and original Irish instrument because most of the social occasions we attended as a family had a real Celtic band, complete with a fiddle, to provide entertainment.

Danny and I operated our businesses (my shoeshine stand and Danny's newspapers) on Patrick's Corner for a good many years. The Shamrock Pub was next door to Chris's Barber Shop and, as we plied our trades, we could hear the melodies of the "auld country" lilt out of the Shamrock's usually open front door. Burly railroaders and longshoremen would lift their voices with their pints and recount the history of Roddy McCorley, who was hanged on the Bridge of Toomb in County Antrim . . . or the fabulously funny lament for Tim Finnegan, who was revived from death by a "noggin' o' whiskey."

Unfortunately, for the Patricks, musical instruments were not easy to come by and we had to resort to our voices for active participation in any musical endeavor. (In later years I would become a passably proficient guitarist and banjo player. I learned these as an adult when I could afford to buy an instrument to practice on. Danny learned to play the piano when his oldest son began taking lessons from Mrs. Flaherty in his Pennsylvania school.)

All of us at least attempted to sing in the choir at St. Columbkille School. Billy and David had beautiful tenor voices which enriched our large ensemble for years. Danny and I, though, got very involved as altar boys and usually served Mass when the choir was scheduled to sing, so we opted for that, instead.

I suppose it was Mama's frequent talking about "the pipes of Kilkenny" that inspired David to go to greater lengths in

181

the annals of Patrick Music. Mama often got a far-away and misty expression in her eyes as she told stories of her girlhood in the rocky county of my forebears.

". . . and the pipes," she would say softly, "the pipes of Kilkenny. How many times I would climb on the thatch of our cottage so that I could hear them more clearly. The jigs, the reels, the laments, and even the dirges sounded so clear in the evening even though they were played from far off. . . ."

I should make it very clear here that I was never a real fan of pipe music. I have always considered the sound to be dissonance when compared to the measured and mathematical precision of more conventional instruments. A few years ago, however, I did enjoy a recording of some British military ensemble playing "Amazing Grace." This record was even very popular on the local radio stations. I think it was when John F. Kennedy was president.

Anyway, David got the bug to play the pipes.

Uncle Michael, Mama's brother, had a set of pipes brought from Ireland in his attic. No one played them and he gladly turned them over to my third-biggest brother. Along with the pipes came a flutelike black instrument which was called a "chanter." This, thank you Saint Cecilia, was what David would use to practice on instead of the full set of pipes.

Mr. O'Grady, who lived in our friend Duffy's apartment on the next block, had been quite a piper in his day, Mama said. David went to see him and he agreed to give David lessons for free. He was glad to see some youngster enthused about taking up an instrument from his native Ireland.

David went to Mr. O'Grady twice each week. He was given an old book with tattered pages covered with black notes. Mr. O'Grady would patiently explain what the notes meant and David would come home and practice them . . . over and over and over and over. After a while, I got kind of used to vacating the bedroom for an hour or so and listening to the faint squeal of the chanter as David, seated on his bed with the book spread out in front of him on the sheet,

182

tootled the big black notes and flicked the tiny grace notes with growing assurance.

From time to time, Mama would look up from her stove and smile that far-off smile which told us that she had returned, if only for an instant, to the thatch-roofed cottage in Kilkenny.

"Mama," I asked her one day, "when will David play the whole thing that he has in the case?"

I was getting tired of the puny sound of the chanter and was now ready to brave the onslaught of the full set of pipes, I guess.

"Mr. O'Grady will tell him when it's time, Seán-o. Ah! It's good to hear the old melodies soundin' again!" she said. "'Brennan on the Moor' never sounded so good as when you haven't heard it for a lifetime."

David's debut on the pipes came suddenly. He came home from Mr. O'Grady's apartment and excitedly told Mama that he was to bring his pipes the next time he went for a lesson.

"Mr. O'Grady made me promise that I wouldn't touch the set of pipes until he told me I could," David said, "and I was true to me promise. I wanted to play on 'em very much but I didn't . . . did I?"

We all said that no he hadn't.

"And now it's time," David went on. "Mr. O'Grady said he's to prepare me for Father Gilhooley's feast day next month!"

Father Gilhooley's first name was Charles. The Feast of St. Charles was November 4th. Father Gilhooley always made a big to-do about his patron saint's Feast Day.

Charles Patrick Gilhooley was slightly older than God, we reasoned. He had been the Pastor of St. Columbkille since its inception and had retired at age seventy-five a good fifteen years ago. He remained at St. Columbkille in retirement and did his best to keep from meddling in the parish affairs, which were now in the able iron fists of Monsignor Hanratty. Father Gilhooley got up early and said the 5:45 A.M. Mass every day of the week, including Sunday.

He was "getting on in years," as the parishioners liked to say, and his eyesight was rapidly failing. To help him with the Mass, he had an altar boy (me, for a long time) hold an old gooseneck desk lamp close to the pages of the Missal. He would bend over the huge book and squint at the bright pages as he muttered his classical Latin prayers almost from memory.

The trick was for the altar boy to get through the whole Mass without tripping on the long extension cord attached to the lamp. Seamus O'Donnell once got the cord so wrapped around his own legs that he tripped from the top step of the altar predella and landed in ignominy at the foot of the steps. The gooseneck lamp followed him, with the bulb bursting like a cannon shot in the quiet church.

Mr. O'Grady thought that it would be a treat for Father Gilhooley to have David play some of the melodies from Ireland on his pipes as the parish gathered to celebrate St. Charles' Feast this particular year.

David practiced very hard for the next few weeks. I don't remember the names of all of the songs he learned, but "The Wearin' of the Green" does stand out in my mind. He was very good . . . for a piper.

The Feast was a great success. David waited outside the hall until the festivities were well started. Mr. O'Grady had given him his own outfit of kilt and jacket in the tartan of the Irish Guard. We dressed David in the boys' bathroom outside the hall and Billy and Kevin stood guard so no one would see him before it was time for him to enter the hall. He looked much older than his fifteen years in that outfit, and I was quite proud to be his baby brother. His red hair (David was the only Patrick with red hair) hung slightly down the front of his forehead and his eyes shone with excitement as he waited for his entrance.

Finally, after two or three hundred years, Mr. O'Grady opened the bathroom door and said it was time.

David walked out and stood dead center in the open double doors leading into the hall. His cap sat at a jaunty angle on his head and even his legs looked manly and strong under the green plaid kilt he wore. The bag of the pipes was tucked securely under his bent left arm, and the "drone" pipes rested on his shoulder, with the plaid ribbon streamer which joined them ruffling in the slight movement of air from the open door.

David was puffing in the long, black tube that jutted out of the bag. It swelled and took form under David's bent arm as the bladder filled with air.

"Keep an even pressure, boy-o," Mr. O'Grady was telling my brother. "Keep a slow march and let the bag do the howlin' fer ye."

"Now?" David asked, the tube resting on the left corner of his mouth.

"Howl 'em, boy-o!" Mr. O'Grady said.

David howled. His left arm jabbed into the bag of air and the drones resting on his shoulder groaned to life. Perhaps they sounded so loud because I was standing right next to them. But it seemed that the air was visibly filled with the reedy chant of the long pipes slung on David's shoulder.

The crowd stopped talking abruptly and turned, as a man, to face the double-door entrance of the hall. David stood for a second, his arm still pressing firmly on the bag. Then his fingers began their tattoo on the slim "chanter" that fell downward from the plaid bag. At the same instant, his left foot began to move and he started into the hall with a majestically slow pace. I even recognized the tune as "All Praise to Saint Patrick" and I, too, swelled with pride in being Irish and the brother of a piper.

Father Gilhooley, seated at the front of the hall next to the table laden with gifts for him from loving parishioners, looked up with an abruptness that startled many around him. He craned his head forward and listened to the sounds of a lifetime ago. A smile broke on his wizened face and his right hand drummed a tempo on the handle of the cane he rested it on.

Monsignor Hanratty was standing in back of Father Gilhooley and reached out a friendly hand and put it on his shoulder. Father Gilhooley was having nothing to do with a hand on his shoulder. He shucked it off as though it were an insect and laboriously rose to his magnificent five-foot two. He leaned his right hand on his cane and stretched his left arm out to welcome the piper who strode slowly towards him.

David reached Father Gilhooley and stopped. The chant continued to pour from the pipes he carried. Father Gilhooley grinned an almost toothless grin and reached out to touch David's arm.

David finished the song and the pipes groaned to a stop.

Father Gilhooley leaned so far forward that several hands reached out as if to catch him if he fell. He didn't. He leaned toward David and said in a creaking voice, "Play me a reel, me buck!"

David played for over an hour. He played reels and jigs, as well as some of the more traditional laments. A crowd had gathered and Mr. O'Grady beamed with pride as his protégé "howled the pipes" for the gathering.

We were all proud of David that night. Many parishioners came up to us to tell us what a fine job our brother had done. Mama was surrounded by acquaintances who all wanted to tell her about how they enjoyed David's piping. Mama was modest but we could tell that she was extremely happy.

This was not, however, the high point in David's piping career. That was to come later and unexpectedly.

It was Christmas Eve, 1949. Our city had been blanketed with a "Christmas card" snow which lay like a soft mantle on our derelict neighborhood, making it look like an out-of-place wonderland. As was our tradition, we attended midnight Mass as a family. Kevin, Danny, and I were altar boys for the Mass and the rest of my brothers sat with Mama in the middle of the large church. After Mass we gathered outside to walk home together.

"Where's David?" Danny asked. He noticed that David was not with Mama, Tommy, and Billy.

"He said he had to run ahead for something," Mama told him, "but he didn't say what it was. Maybe some sort of surprise for us, I'll be thinkin'."

We walked home slowly. Danny and I made some snowballs to throw at signs and Mama cautioned us not to hit anyone's windows, "especially on the holy night of Christmas Eve."

As we approached our apartment Mama stopped dead in her tracks. We all stopped. Her head lifted to the sky and she listened intently. Then we all heard it.

From far above us we heard the distinct drone of the bagpipe, then the skirl as the chanter picked up a melody.

Mama's eyes clouded and we all looked at her face, which was lighted by the single streetlight in front of her. The sounds were high and clear.

David was standing on the roof of our apartment, four floors above the street. He was wearing the kilt of the Irish Guard and was piping the carol "What Child Is This?"

Neighbors walking home from Mass in back of us stopped, too. Their happy chatter faded and they stood enthralled with our family as Mama's third son stood high above in the cold, piping a tune to the King.

People in the apartment opened their windows and craned heads out. No one was complaining, though. Not even the Golnicks or the Feldmans, who really weren't celebrating this evening. They, too, were delighted with David's gift to us all.

The song stopped and we started towards our apartment door. Then the piping began again. This time it was different and the gift was unmistakable. David was softly piping "Kathleen Mavourneen" . . . the song Daddy had courted Mama with. Her name was Kathleen.

Tommy handed Mama his fresh, white handkerchief.

David played on many occasions after that. He even piped Father Gilhooley to his grave, marching at the front of the funeral procession piping a slow march as the old priest was laid to his rest.

He piped for many parish occasions and was frequently asked to pipe at weddings, for which he usually earned five dollars.

187

I'm still not a fan of the bagpipe. One of my own sons is, but thankfully plays the drums in a makeshift rock n' roll group comprised of his equally semi-talented friends. But I was a fan for a few moments a couple of times in my life.

There's not a Christmas goes by that I don't envision our old street with its covering of fresh snow. I still feel the cold air nipping my face and the woolen scarf up around my ears. . . . I feel my neck straining backward as I look to the sky.

I suppose the Christmas star was shining brightly over our apartment that night. It was a very holy night, indeed. But I didn't look for the star. I looked for a piper and saw my brother, kilt blowing in the wind and clouds of vapor pouring from his nostrils as he gave us . . . and Mama . . . our present.

It was beautiful music, indeed.

"David?" I said from my bed. Danny stirred, too. He, like me, was still awake that Christmas Eve. His warmth felt good next to me as we huddled under our feather blanket.

"What, Seán-o?"

"I think your music was very nice tonight."

"Thanks, Seán-o."

"That's because he was pipin' love." Kevin added.

"I hope you'll all remember that when I'm practicin' next time!" David said.

We settled down and were soon asleep.

Yes, I'm sure the Christmas star was shining.

The Warrior

"... my hand will be constantly with him,
he will be able to rely on my arm.
No enemy will be able to outwit him,
no wicked man to worst him,
I myself will crush his opponents,
I will strike dead all who hate him.
With my faithfulness and love,
his fortunes shall rise in my name.
I will give him control of the sea,
complete control of the rivers.
He will invoke me, 'My father,
my God, and rock of my safety.'"

Psalm 89:21-26

THREE PATRICKS WORE the uniform of their country, all in the United States Navy. Three Patricks stayed to do battle with poverty and ignorance on their own soil and in the uniform of the common man. All served with honor.

Tommy was the only Patrick to experience real battle. He was in the navy during the Korean conflict and was stationed off the coast of that peninsula on a ship of war—an aircraft carrier, to be exact.

All the Patricks who served in the armed forces were worried about and thought about by the rest of the clan. However, Tommy got the most attention because he was actually under fire from a sworn enemy while the rest of us served during less hazardous times.

We rejoiced greatly when Tommy came home to stay because he returned uninjured and none the worse for wear. At least as far as we could see.

War is an insanity. It is truly the work of the Evil One running rampant on Earth. Except in the most unusual and horrible of circumstances, it has no validity, no logical forethought, nor consequential justification at all.

We never thought much about the philosophical aspects

189

of war when we were young. All of us had lived through the inconveniences of World War II: the lack of certain items, the shortages of fuel and certain foods, the OPA ration booklet which Mama carried to the store with the tiny stamps to be torn out and handed to the clerk as we paid our bill. . . . We even did some very positive things in our neighborhood. We collected tin cans and crushed them so that they could be turned in to assist in the War Effort (as this type of service was called). We saved the nubs of soap and saved grease and all sorts of other things that the adults would convert somewhere so that soldiers could be saved.

The country was driven during the Second World War, caught up in some sort of frenzy of patriotism and we, like all the rest, were part of it. We were pretty removed from the "fray" and didn't really realize that people were being bombed and torn to bits as we cheered our troops on.

I remember V-J Day more than V-E Day. I guess that V-E day just kind of slipped by my memory.

But V-J Day was a memory that I'll never forget.

I don't remember much of the forewarnings. I can recall, however, that early in the evening the adults were gathering in groups and talking about the surrender. Then there was a long, long pause when they found out, via the radio, that no surrender had actually been effected.

We all stayed close to our radios and Danny and I fell asleep in our underwear in front of ours. The Feldmans and the O'Malleys were in our apartment because their radios didn't work. There was an awful lot of movement around but Danny and I slept anyway.

In the late hours it happened. We were awakened by cheers from the people in the apartment and outside of it. It was a warm summer night and all of the windows were open.

"It's over!" was the shout and everyone was hugging everyone else. Tommy ran outside and rode up and down the street on his bicycle shouting the phrase at the top of his lungs. Some of the Kennedy kids got ahold of a batch of flares from the railroad and were posting them at the ends

190

of the street. It was a wild, wild night.

Danny and I ran out in our underwear and were shouting with all the rest. Then, as if we had heard a signal, we returned to the apartment stoop where Mama and the other "cliff dwellers" were gathering. It grew strangely quiet in the immediate area but shouts, shotguns, and cheers resounded in the distance.

"Gather here, boys," Mama said, and we all gathered around her. Mr. O'Malley, whose son Connell was in the army and stationed somewhere on some island, was standing on the top step. We all looked at him as if drawn to him by some invisible, irresistible force.

"I think, my friends, this is a time to thank our Maker and Protector . . ." he said.

The silence was eerie. It seemed as though even the distant celebration had been upheld for the moment. We stared at Mr. O'Malley, who was trembling.

Mrs. O'Malley held her husband's elbow. "Lead us, Kermit," she said.

"Almighty God," he began with a strong voice, "we thank you for the protection you have held over us. We thank you . . ." His voice became suddenly—very suddenly—small and distant as the tears began to flood from his eyes and his shoulders sagged. Mrs. O'Malley held him with both of her arms as he sank to sit on the top step.

". . . we thank you. We thank you . . . we thank you. . . ." The sobs shook his entire body, but we knew very well what message he conveyed for all of us in his prayer. The eloquence of his tears was sufficient language for our purpose.

Tommy, being the oldest, was the first Patrick to go into the service. After he graduated from Holy Redeemer he went to work for a while at the butcher shop, but never intended to make that his life's work. Instead, seeing the writing on the wall because of what was beginning in Korea, he elected to join the navy and get his service obligation over with and also be able to finance at least part of his schooling through the G.I. Bill.

Billy had just graduated from Holy Redeemer when

Tommy announced his intention of joining up. I guess he felt that Billy could hold things together while we went about the business of growing up and all that. Mama was a bit concerned, but knew that it was the right thing for him to do. She was very much aware, however, of Korea.

Tommy never tried to hide the fact that, while he was overseas, he was experiencing hostilities. We were glad that his letters did not say "everything is fine and I'm really enjoying myself." After all, we did know that Jerry Feldman had given his life there and would all too soon be shocked by Duffy's death in that same place.

Tommy's ship was hit several times during his tour, but he was never injured—at least not physically. His letters, although upbeat and generally pleasant, carried an undercurrent of profound displeasure and disillusionment. Tommy had never experienced man's apparently inherent hostility towards man before.

"I find it hard," he wrote in one letter to us all, "to understand just why we are here and why we are fighting these people. They really pose no real threat to any of us. Kev, you'd really like most of them because they take their sports very seriously and enjoy playing the game for the sake of the game. Even you, Mama, would be impressed with the attitude the people have regarding their work. Most of them work from sunup to sundown without a complaint. I bet you'd like to see some of your sons so diligent!"

After his tour of duty in Korea Tommy spent several months Stateside preparing to be discharged and returned to us for good. He had a couple of opportunities to travel home for short periods of time, and we enjoyed seeing him. He was, however, somewhat different.

One warm evening Tommy was home because Mary O'Leary had had to do something with her family and he had nowhere else in particular to go. We (Danny, Tommy, and I) ended up sitting on the stoop enjoying the first cool that we had felt that day.

"So, how did it go today at Patrick's Corner?" Tommy asked.

"I sold out me papers and Seán-o shined four shoes," Danny told him. "I'm up to a hundred papers a night now and hardly ever have any left."

It was nice making small talk with our biggest brother. He was dressed in his ordinary clothes and it was just like it used to be.

"What's it like, Tommy, the war?" I asked him innocently.

"You don't want to know, Seán-o," Tommy said after a slight pause. "War ain't something I like to talk about."

There was a longer pause and Tommy seemed to be thinking of something far away. Perhaps he was hearing the bullets striking the metal plates on his aircraft carrier. . . . He seemed lost in his own world for a time.

"Sorry, Tommy . . ." I began to say.

"Don't be sorry, brother. War is just somethin' that seems to be . . . kind of . . . well, dirty. I don't really want to think about it anymore and I'm glad that I'm on my way out."

"You didn't like bein' in the navy?" Danny chimed in.

"Oh, I love it, the navy," Tommy said quickly. "I've learned a lot and they treat me fine. It's the damned fighting I don't like!"

We were both a little surprised by Tommy's vulgarity. I guess it showed on our faces.

"It's scary an' it's plain stupid!" Tommy went on vehemently. "A bunch of grown men droppin' bombs on each other and shootin' guns and playin' like the cowboys and Indians. . . . It's a damned stupid way to go!"

Tommy stood up abruptly and went into the apartment leaving Danny and I sitting on the stoop. We kind of looked at each other dumbly.

Danny and I went to Irish Kennedy's for a while to watch Morey Amsterdam on the Kennedys' television set. When it was over we went home. Mama was down talking to Mrs. O'Malley and the rest of the guys were doing important things somewhere else. It was a sort of dull, disquieting evening all around.

"I'm turnin' in early, Seán-o," Danny said. "I've been yawnin' since we were on the Corner this afternoon."

"Me, too," I agreed. We both headed into the bedroom and found Tommy lying on top of the bed just staring at the ceiling.

"'Night, Tommy," I said as I started undressing for bed.

"'Night, guys," Tommy answered from his prone position. "Don't forget your prayers."

"'K, Tommy," I said and Danny and I knelt beside the bed for our nightly prayers. We usually prayed together and aloud since we were kids. Three "Our Fathers," three "Hail, Marys," three "Glory Be's," and the Act of Contrition. Then we said the part of the Psalm written on the sheet of notebook paper that Danny got from on top of the dresser.

". . . and for our brother, Tommy: '. . . my hand will be constantly with him, he will be able to rely on my arm. No enemy will be able to outwit him, no wicked man to worst him. I myself will crush his opponents, I will strike dead all who hate him . . .'"

"Hey! What's this you guys are sayin'?" Tommy sat up on the bed.

"A Psalm," Danny answered, turning his head to Tommy. "Mama gave it to us to say when you went in the navy. We all say it every night for ye."

"Cor!" Tommy said. "I knew ye prayed for me, but I didn't think you'd be singin' a Psalm for your brother."

Danny turned back to the paper.

"'With my faithfulness and love, his fortunes shall rise in my name. I will give him control of the sea, complete control of the rivers. He will invoke me, "My father, my God, and rock of my safety."'"

We rose up and climbed into bed. We said goodnight to Tommy and soon slept.

That Sunday it was time for Tommy to take the long bus ride back to his base. He still had several months to go before he was to be home for good. We all went, as usual, to the bus station to see him off. Mary O'Leary went with us, too. Tommy really looked trim and nice in his blue uniform.

Mary and Mama went over to look at some magazines while we were waiting for the bus. Kev was watching some men playing the pinball machines and David, Billy, Danny, and I sat in the uncomfortable chairs with Tommy.

"So, Dan-o," Tommy said, "you guys all pray that Psalm every night for me?"

"Sure, Tommy. Mama thought that we needed somethin' a little more official because of what you're doin' now. Father O'Toole found that prayer for her to give us."

"Thanks, guys," Tommy said to us all. "I really appreciate you guys sayin' that for me."

We all kind of self-consciously nodded that it was O.K. and we didn't feel put-upon to say a Psalm for our brother.

"And, you know," he went on, "I went down to talk to the Monsignor meself while I was home. I told him about how I was feelin' an' everything. You know what he said?"

We said that no, we didn't know.

"He said that it was O.K. to feel the way I do. He said that from as far as we can go back in history man's been fightin' against man and that there has to be someone to stand up and do the battle even if they hate it so the evil doesn't win out over the good."

Tommy was speaking very swiftly.

"He said that every generation has got to have people who will do this work even if they hate it so bad that it tastes sour in their mouths. But that it has to be done."

Tommy paused for air, but none of us said anything. Mama and Mary were standing there listening to him, too. Even Kevin had stopped watching the man play pinball and stood at Tommy's chair with his hand on his shoulder.

"So you see it's O.K. that I do this thing and that I still don't have to like it. It's just something that's got to be done and I'm one of those who is picked to do it."

He fished a small folded paper out of his trouser pocket, which was under the bottom of his middie blouse.

"I told him of your Psalm. He said that it was good and that the Psalms say things in a way to make us take notice. He even gave me a bit of a Psalm for meself."

He passed the paper to Mama. She looked at it for a moment and then handed it back to him. He looked at it carefully and lovingly. Then he read from Psalm 107.

"'They that go down to the sea in ships, that do business in great waters, these see the works of the Lord, and his wonders in the deep.'"

As I said, Tommy was the only one of the three of us who actually saw battle. He spoke of it from time to time, mostly to answer questions we had about his experiences. But he never glorified it. It was, for him, a difficult job that he was supposed to do and he was very glad when it was over and done with.

"Seán-o?" Danny said that night as we prepared to fall asleep.

"Hmmmmm?"

"It's just a job he does, Tommy."

"Mmmmmmm. I know. He told us."

"I sure hope I don't get picked for a job like that."

"Mama says we should be prayin' hard for peace," I told my brother.

"Tommy hates it, the war part."

"If they decide to have a war when we're old enough, maybe we'll all tell 'em to fight it themselves."

"That'd teach 'em."

"'Night, Dan-o."

"'Night, brother."

196

The Orangeman

IN OUR DAY it was not a common occurrence to have heard of, much less to have known, a "preacher's kid." We were Irish Catholic and lived in a predominantly Irish and Catholic neighborhood. The few non-Irish were considered to be acceptable, and the fewer non-Catholics were staunchly prayed for and considered to be less fortunate, but decent friends.

When we said "clergyman" we meant, with almost zero exceptions, one of the priests from the St. Columbkille parish. On occasion we might have been referring to the bishop or even, on very rare occasions, the pope. Never, in even our most far-fetched dreams, would we have been referring to a married man.

Nonetheless, it must be said that Martin Tracy was a clergyman. He was the pastor, or minister, of Hardin Presbyterian Church on Hardin Street. An Irishman, he was, to put it bluntly, an Orangeman.

As I reflect back I am very thankful that we—my brothers and I—were raised during the more "fun" years of the ongoing difficulties between Ireland and Northern Ireland . . . that land of six counties stolen from Ireland by the dread "King Billy," who was never held in great esteem by the true Irish. We were steadfastly "green" through and through. We sang the IRA songs and shouted the chant of "Up the long ladder and down the short rope, to hell with King Billy and God bless the pope. . . ." We did not discuss the few "wayward" O'Hickeys or Patricks who, in the course of history, had ventured into the Northern counties and remained there, presumably "Orange" and Protestant.

But . . . we didn't carry it to the extremes that later developed.

Was it Sheridan who wrote that "Ireland is a land of happy wars and sad love songs . . . ?" That may have been true, at one time.

Although Martin Tracy was in fact the spiritual leader of a local church, he was, in the estimation of the great majority of the neighborhood's "true" Irishmen—as we considered ourselves and our friends—all that a clergyman should not be. He was Protestant; he was married; he was "Orange"; and he was a father. He didn't even dress like a clergyman should. No Roman collar, no black suit, no pipe or straw hat like Bing Crosby wore in "Going My Way."

The problem was that Dennis Tracy, Reverend Tracy's oldest child and only son, was a friend of Danny's.

I really don't remember how Dennis and Danny got to be friends. In fact, Danny doesn't even remember how they met. They were sort of casual friends . . . you know, the waving kind, before they really started to associate and do things together.

Since Dennis was Danny's friend, he became my friend, too. Danny and I were like peas in a pod for most of our early lives and what one did, the other did as well. So, a friend of Danny's was a friend of mine. And, if the truth be told, I really didn't mind having Dennis as a friend. He was a pretty neat kid.

It took Mama some time before she really accepted Dennis as a part of Danny's and my life. Mama wasn't truly prejudiced against anyone. At least we never thought so. But, an Orangeman was an Orangeman and needed to be treated with some suspicion.

"I don't see why, Daniel," Mama said one day to my next older brother, "you'll be needin' to take up with an Orange boy when you've plenty of friends right around here."

"But, Mama, he's a friend no matter what else there is about him!" Danny remonstrated.

That was about the extent of Mama's fuss. Eventually she let Danny or me bring Dennis home just like all of our other friends, where he blended into the woodwork like the rest. It just took a little longer for that to happen.

Even now I hear stories of how "wild" preacher's kids are. The reputation may or may not be deserved. The few whom I know are seemingly normal children of seemingly normal parents. True, they may conduct secret rituals in their attics, or bury dead animals in their back yards by the light of the moon . . . or they may be as normal as you or I, for what that's worth.

Dennis was anything but wild. He was a rather shy boy who, being an only son and one of two children, did not have the experience of having older brothers to teach him all about everything essential to growing up.

Danny was thoroughly incensed, for example, to learn that Dennis had never learned to swim, a skill Danny equated with walking or being able to chew food. For a boy of fourteen to have never swung from a suspended Tarzan swing and, from there, plunged headlong into the deeply dredged riverbend, was unthinkable and he sought to correct this hole in Dennis's education forthwith.

My brothers and I used to swim in the polluted Courtney River, which bridled our city like a horseshoe, at least a couple of times a week in the summer months. I had learned to swim there when I was five years old. I still remember Billy tossing me into the water next to where Tommy stood up to his neck in case something "went wrong," and watching me dog paddle back to him time after time until they were satisfied that I was floatable and would not drown. By the time I was in first grade I could hold my own on the Tarzan swing, which we hung from a tall oak growing on the riverbank.

Kevin, Danny, and I hatched our plan and didn't tell Dennis what we were going to do when we led him, unsuspecting, to the banks of the Courtney on a sweltering July afternoon. "Our" spot was secluded from the road by a very thick grove of oak and maple trees. The water, although it was rapidly becoming ever more polluted by the industry on the banks of the river, looked cool and inviting.

"But I don't know HOW to swim," Dennis pleaded when we informed him that he, like us, was going for a dip.

He had every excuse known to man. He was afraid he'd get pinkeye; we assured him nobody had yet contracted that disease from the Courtney and that only the chlorinated city pool (which cost 10 cents to swim in) had pinkeye

199

germs. He was afraid that he'd get water in his ear and that he'd lose his hearing; we told him that you got water out of your ear by jumping up and down and striking the side of your head with the flat of your hand. He had heard that you got polio from swimming; old wives' tales, we countered. He had no swimming suit; we didn't either, but that had never stopped us from swimming before. He had no towel and would catch cold; in 97-degree weather? we asked. Anyway, the sun and warm breeze would dry him in seconds.

Eventually we got ourselves, and Dennis, undressed and Kevin, Danny, and I waded out into the water. Dennis stood for a few minutes looking horribly self-conscious and uncomfortable. He kept looking over his shoulder as though he was expecting someone to pop out of the bushes.

"The bugger's scared someone's gonna' see him in the raw!" Kevin whispered to Danny. We were in water up to our necks by this time.

"Watch this," Danny hissed to Kevin and me.

"Dennis! Girls comin'!" he shouted.

Dennis jerked upright and paused for only a second. Then he splashed out into the chest-high water so fast he almost had a wake following him!

We were laughing when he reached us and Danny splashed water at me. I splashed Dennis and soon we were all splashing and having a great time.

Kevin taught Dennis how to relax in the water and Dennis caught on quickly. Before we left that afternoon, Dennis was swinging from our Tarzan swing like an expert.

From that afternoon on Dennis was a frequent companion on our swimming escapades in the Courtney. Every so often someone or other would yell "GIRLS!" and Dennis would just about jump out of his Orange Irish skin, but aside from that we had a real good time whenever we went.

Dennis' father, though, was having a difficult time of it. Being Irish and Protestant was not an easy thing in our town. Prejudice flows in many directions, and Martin Tracy was drowning in the midst of it. He was not acceptable to the

200

Irish because of his Protestantism and not acceptable to the Protestants because of being Irish. His small congregation was dwindling and the offerings given at the Sunday service were certainly not enough to support Pastor Tracy, to say nothing of Mrs. Tracy, Dennis, and his sister.

Just as Duffy had become a part of the Patrick family because of his friendship with Kevin, so Dennis Tracy became a part of our lives because of his friendship with Danny and, I like to think, me. Even Mama took a liking to this quiet, good-natured boy who never failed to ask her how she was and how did she like the weather or the season or whatever was important for the moment.

Like Duffy, too, it took some convincing to allow us to "help" Dennis in small ways. If asking him to share a meal or anything like that appeared to be an offer of charity, Dennis would refuse—politely, of course, but he would refuse. We didn't have a lot to offer, but Tommy was now working full time and Billy and David had part-time jobs which brought in enough extra so that Mama was able to make sure that we had substantial meals. We were up to meat twice a week with the boys' helping out.

Even at my young age, I was able to see certain things about people. You don't live in a large family without learning about people. I was fairly observant for a thirteen-year-old.

It impressed me that Mr. Tracy could keep a cheerful disposition through all of the difficulty he must have been having. We would see him from time to time in the neighborhood and he would always smile and ask how we were doing.

Some of the neighbors, however, were openly hostile to this gentle man. I suppose that many of them had suffered from the conflict in the Old Country and had personal reasons for not liking an "Orangeman," but I would have found it difficult to transfer this to a person like Mr. Tracy.

On the other hand, when I think back I remember how hostile we were to any Orientals after the Second World War. It took a long time for me, for example, to realize that

1) all Orientals are not Japanese, 2) all Japanese were not enemies, and 3) that war is the most unreasonable type of behavior man can come up with and it carries with it irrational, illogical, and most hateful consequences in terms of human response.

Most of the Presbyterians from Hardin Street Presbyterian Church had "gone over" to Faith Presbyterian on Coleman Street because of Mr. Tracy's being Irish. In a way, I suppose, I took that as an insult against the Irish and against myself and my family.

We discussed this one evening at supper when Dennis was not there. Mama listened to Danny and me griping about the gross injustice dealt the Tracy family because of their Irish heritage. Tommy was even fairly vocal about it.

"Damn shame!" he spouted. Mama told him to watch his mouth, but you could tell that it had set her to thinking.

"I don't like it!" Billy said, emphatically. He rose from the table and paced back and forth by the stove as he carried on a monologue with himself . . . and, indirectly, with us.

"Just because the bloke's an Irishman those people get on him and treat him like he's got no worth. Mr. Tracy's a fine man. I've talked to him from time to time and he's always interested in what I've got to say . . . comes to the store and always has a friendly word for all of us. Tommy's right, it's a shame."

I know what was going through all of our minds. I remembered the remarks we, ourselves, had made not too long ago about Orangemen and other groups. We were not without fault in this category, either.

We were good talkers but not very experienced doers. Deep inside we knew that something needed to be done but didn't know what or how. Even Mama was very quiet after that conversation and her sometimes caustic remarks about the Orange Irish disappeared from her conversation.

Nothing much changed for several weeks. Like I said, we were good talkers but not very good doers. Then, one afternoon, Mama met Mr. Tracy at the grocery store.

Mama made several trips each week to the small grocer's

near St. Columbkille. Our food supply depended largely on the income for the week, which varied depending on Mama's cleaning jobs and the amount generated by the older boys. She rather enjoyed these trips, too. It was a type of socializing which was common among our people.

Mr. Tracy was there to buy a few items for his family table when he and Mama met near the potatoes.

"Hello, Mrs. Patrick!" Mr. Tracy said.

"Ah! Reverend Tracy. How are you today?" Mama responded. The big thing was that she called him "Reverend" . . . loudly enough for other customers to hear.

"Fine, thank you. I trust that you and your boys are well?"

"Fit as fiddles. Not too many germs can get through the crowd in me kitchen, Reverend. Your Dennis can tell you that sometimes we have to walk sideways to pass each other."

"Yes, Dennis enjoys his friendship with your boys, especially with Danny. Having good friends has surely helped him get over his shyness."

"Dennis tells us that your family is from Armagh?"

"My father, Mrs. Patrick. I was born here, but my father came from Armagh and spoke often of the Old Country."

"And Mrs. Tracy, is she born here, too?"

"Ah, no. Maura is from a place called Hy Maine, near Sligo."

"Oh yes, the coaleries. I know the place well. I'd like very much to meet Mrs. Tracy and talk with her about the Old Country."

"I'm sure that she'd like that, Mrs. Patrick."

"Reverend Tracy, tomorrow I'm fixin' cod and we always have plenty of that. Perhaps you and your family could join us for our supper? It's not fancy but Dennis seems to enjoy it very much."

Mr. Tracy was surprised. It probably showed on his face because Mama rattled on, which was not usually her way, so as to give him time to get his astonishment under control.

"Such a nice boy, too. It's a good example he sets with his table manners for my boys!"

"Why, thank you, Mrs. Patrick. I will ask Maura and send word with Dennis if that's alright."

"Fine, Reverend. I do hope she can come. All of you—your daughter, too."

Mama left the store with many persons staring at her. She nodded to each and shared a word or two about the weather with a few and walked back to our apartment.

That evening Dennis showed up and, a little breathlessly, explained that his father and mother would be happy to come to our apartment for dinner the next night. He joined us at our table and dug into the scrambled eggs with the gusto of someone who belonged there.

Dinner the next night was fun. We were very, very crowded, but no one seemed to mind. As was typical in a potentially tense social situation, Tommy kept up a steady stream of jokes generally aimed at Billy, who purposely fell for all of the punch lines expected of the "straight man" in a comedy team. Kev was all over the place, helping Mama carry bowls and platters to the table. Dennis sat on the long bench between Danny and me and his sister, Rose, sat next to my left arm. She was very quiet but seemed to enjoy it, anyway.

After supper Danny and I had dishes and Dennis jumped in to help. Mama visited with Mrs. Tracy at the kitchen table while Mr. Tracy and Rose sat in the living room listening to David retell the story of how he got interested in playing the pipes. It was a fine evening and everyone ended up feeling very much at ease.

Because of the warm evening, many of the apartment dwellers were sitting on the stoop outside when the Tracys took their leave. Mr. Tracy nodded to them and smiled. A couple of them returned his greeting and no one muttered any insults.

I don't know how much Mama's invitation helped. Maybe it was only coincidental timing, but things began to change a bit for the Tracys. The church stabilized and, though it never had a large congregation, became a very active church, with programs for its young and even a ladies' club

204

which had a nice bazaar in the fall. Mr. Tracy was greeted politely by Orange and Green alike and most of the invectives hurled at him for his Orange heritage disappeared. They became, like us, a part of the neighborhood.

Dennis remained close friends with Danny and with me.

When Danny went to college to become an accountant, Dennis went to another college to become, like his father, a Presbyterian minister. I was out of the navy and in college myself when he was ordained to the ministry. Our whole family went to his father's church one Sunday morning to hear him preach his first sermon after his ordination. It was very good, too. It was all about First Corinthians, chapter thirteen.

"'. . . and, in the end, there will be three things that last: Faith, Hope, and Love. And the greatest of these is Love!'"

When Danny married several years later he was married in St. Columbkille church. Monsignor Hanratty was dead, so the "new" pastor, Monsignor Fahey, celebrated the occasion. In the infant spirit of the new ecumenism beginning in the Roman Catholic Church, the Monsignor permitted Danny to invite Dennis to co-celebrate his wedding, and Dennis said several prayers over the beaming couple. Reverend Martin Tracy and his wife were also present for the big day.

Dennis looked so good and holy standing in his black academic gown (which, I believe, is traditional garb for Presbyterian ministers) as he prayed in a strong and loving voice over my brother and his bride. As best man, I stood on the side a bit and could watch everything carefully.

Although most of my attention was on my next older brother and his bride, my eyes strayed from time to time to Dennis, who was standing next to Monsignor Fahey. While the Monsignor prayed, Dennis bowed his head and closed his eyes. I knew that Dennis was very sincerely praying for Danny because he genuinely loved him—almost as much as his baby brother did. Suddenly, I sniggered a bit and put my hand over my mouth as if to stifle a cough.

After the service and the reception line, Danny and his

bride got into Tommy's car to head for the reception at the Legion Hall. I was starting to help Mama into my own car when Dennis came up in back of me.

"Seán-o! What were you laughin' at in there?"

"Nothin', Dennis. Nothin' at all!"

"C 'mon, Seán-o, I know you better than that!"

"OK, Den. If you must know I was laughin' at the same thing I laughed at when you preached your first sermon."

"I didn't know you laughed then—what was it all about? Did I do something funny?"

"Den, I know you've got the dignity of the cloth and all that and I love you very much . . . but both times I looked at you and the same vision popped into my head."

"Like?"

"Like a scrawny Irish kid standin' buck naked on the banks of the Courtney scared out of his wits that someone would pop out of the bushes and catch a glimpse of his skinny arse!"

Dennis reached over my shoulders and hugged me to him. Affection fairly glowed in his eyes.

"We've come a long way, brother," he said.

I kept silent but I agreed. Over my friend's shoulder I could see Monsignor Fahey on the steps of St. Columbkille laughing at something Reverend Martin Tracy had just said to him. They were both laughing.

". . . and, in the end, there will be three things that last: Faith, Hope, and Love. And the greatest of these is Love!"

Amen.